Text Copyright 2016 Mark A. Ashford Consulting Inc.
All Rights Reserved

Paperback ISBN **978-1-990876-14-1**

eBook ISBN 978-1-990876-13-4

1. Introduction

Shamanism is the oldest religion on the planet!

In human existence it predates current day organized religions by many millennia. Shamans are traditional healers, guides and protectors. They are a universal expression of the interaction between people and the natural and supernatural worlds. European cave paintings and carvings showing shaman date from the Paleolithic era and in 2016, a 12,000-year-old grave of a female shaman has been uncovered in Israel.

Shamans have played an essential role in the defence of the psychic integrity of their community for thousands of years.

In a general way, it can be said that shamanism defends life, health, fertility, and the world of "light," against death, diseases, sterility, disaster and the world of "darkness." Fundamental to shamans struggle against what we could call the powers of evil. Shamans cannot foresee the future but also change the outcome. As an example, shamans can find out where food or game is located in the community, or avert threats to the community. This is a vital difference between shamanism and clairvoyance.[1]

We will look more deeply into the shaman world of Mongolia, Siberia, and Tibet and the other religious expressions, such as Bon and Buddhism.

This is the book that is complementary to my books on Reiki and other aspects of Shamanism; there is a direct link between the Shaman's Helping Spirits and Reiki Guides that help Reiki practitioners bring healing and comfort to people today.

Connect with our Private Facebook group to learn more about Reiki. Click here.

Subscribe to our newsletter to learn more about Reiki and Shamanism. Click here

Enjoy.

Mark Ashford, MSc,
Usui Tibetan Reiki Master and Teacher [IARP], Registered Reiki Teacher and Practitioner [CRA]
https://www.markaashford.com
information@markaashford.com

---

[1] https://www.energy-shifter.com/shamanism-and-spiritual-techniques.html, Shamanism,andsoulretrieval-SpiritualHouseCleansing.

Table of contents

1. INTRODUCTION 2
2. TABLE OF FIGURES 6
3. SHAMANISM 7
    - 3.1. The Shaman Calling 9
4. TNGRI, TENGRI 11

FIGURE 1. TREE OF LIFE. IMAGE BY DMYTRO FROM PIXABAY 13

    - 4.1. Tengri Shamanism 15
5. CONTEMPORARY TENGRISM 17
6. ANCESTOR WORSHIP 19
7. SHAMAN 21
    - 7.1. Healer and Guide 22
    - 7.2. Oracle 23
    - 7.1. Continuity 24
    - 7.2. Protector 25
    - 7.3. Other Traditions of Shaman Selection 25
    - 8. Soul 28
    - 8.1. Dictionary Definition 28
    - 8.2. Etymology 28
    - 8.3. Incorporeal Essence 29
    - 8.4. Human Body 29
    - 8.5. Other Bodies 30
    - 8.6. Spirit 30
    - 8.4. Atman–Hinduism 31
    - 8.5. Theological Soul 31
    - 8.6. Where Is the Soul in the Physical Body? 32
    - 8.7. Ensoulment 33
9. SHAMANIC SOUL 34
    - 9.1. Shamanism and Animism 34
    - 9.2. Bon Sarma 34
    - 9.3. Mixed Bon 35
    - 9.4. Bo Murgel 35
    - 9.5. Dzogchen 35
10. SIGNS OF SOUL LOSS 36
11. SOUL RETRIEVAL 37
    - 11.1. Other Bodies 38
    - 11.2. Spirit 39
12. SOUL LOSS AND RETRIEVAL OF ELEMENTAL ENERGIES 40
13. ELEMENT RETRIEVAL 43
14. SOUL RETRIEVAL–AN EXAMPLE 44
15. SOUL CHANNELS 46
16. DIFFERENCE BETWEEN SPIRIT AND SOUL 49
17. SHAMAN V'S MEDIUMS 50

18.	SHAMAN V'S A MEDICINE MAN	52
19.	SHAMAN V'S A WITCH DOCTOR	55
20.	BLACK, WHITE AND YELLOW SHAMAN	57
21.	BLACK SHAMAN	58
22.	WHITE SHAMAN	59
23.	YELLOW SHAMAN	60
24.	LEVELS OF CONSCIOUSNESS	62
25.	SACRED DIRECTIONS	62
25.1.	Five Elements	63
25.2.	Earth	64
25.3.	Water	65
25.4.	Fire	65
25.5.	Air	66
25.6.	Space	66
25.7.	Imbalance of Elements	66
25.8.	Five Elements and Sacred Directions	67
25.9.	At Birth	67
25.10.	Sentient Being in Each Element	68
25.11.	Eight Classes of Being	68
25.12.	Four Levels of Guests	69
25.10.	Making offering to the Guests	71
25.11.	Chang-Bu Offering	71
25.12.	The Twelve Astrological Signs and their Directions	72
26.	ALTERED STATES OF CONSCIOUSNESS [ASC]	74
26.2.	Shaman's Drum	78
26.3.	Bon Shamanic Music and Buddhism	78
26.4.	Bells and Cymbals	78
26.5.	Dreams	79
26.6.	Other Thoughts	79
27.	TIBETAN BOOK OF THE DEAD.	80
27.2.	Origins.	80
28.	SIX BARDO STATES	84
28.4.	Bardo Thodol and additional states	86
29.	SACRED PLACES	88
29.1.	Mount Kailash	88
30.	Bon	89
30.1.	Hindus	89
30.2.	Jains	89
30.3.	Potala Palace:	91
30.4.	Jokhang Temple	92
30.5.	Norbulingka:	92
30.6.	Drepung Monastery	93
31.	BON RELIGION	94
31.1.	Primary Differences Between Buddhism and Bon	96
31.2.	Shamanism and Animism	96

32.	**SHAMANISM: RITUALS AND SPIRITUALITY**	98
32.1.	Drums and Drumstick	100
32.2.	Songs	100
32.3.	Dance	101
32.4.	Costumes	102
32.5.	Head Band and Head Dress	102
32.6.	Cloak	102
32.7.	Foot Wear	103
32.8.	Alters and Shrines	103
33.	**SHAMANIC MIRRORS**	103
34.	**SHAMANISM: CHANGING PERCEPTIONS**	107
35.	**PERSECUTION OF SHAMAN**	110
35.1.	Religious Persecution in Tibet	110
35.2.	History	110
35.3.	Shamans	111
35.4.	Current Threats	112
36.	**ASIAN AND EUROPEAN SHAMANISM**	114
36.1.	Humming Shamanism	114
36.1.	Japan	115
36.2.	S. Korea	115
36.3.	Malaysia	116
36.4.	Mongolia	116
36.5.	Philippines	118
36.6.	Siberia and North Asia	119
36.7.	Vietnam	121
36.8.	Other Asian traditions	121
36.9.	Europe	122
37.	**BIBLIOGRAPHY**	123

2. Table of Figures

Figure 1. Tree of Life. Image by Dmytro from Pixabay 13

3. Shamanism

hamanism is not unique to any specific part of the world; it is a spiritual tradition that connects humanity with the natural world and engages us with the other realms of existence in which souls and spirits exist that affect our physical world.

Geographically, evidence of shamans appears in cave paintings in the Czech Republic dating from the Paleolithic[2] era. And 12,000 old graves of shaman women[3] have been found in Northern Israel. In this book, we will concentrate on shamanism as it was and still is expressed in Mongolia[4], Siberia[5], Buryatia[6], Tibet[7], and Nepal[8].

The word shaman probably derives from the Manchu-Tungus[9] word šaman, meaning "one who knows." The word shaman may also have originated from the Evenki word šamán, most likely from the southwestern dialect spoken by the Sym Evenki peoples. The Tungusic term was subsequently adopted by Russians interacting with the Indigenous peoples in Siberia. It is found in the memoirs of the exiled Russian churchman Avvakum.[10]

The Mongols universe is more than the three dimensions we can visualize. It includes spiritual worlds and realms above and below this physical one and the past, present and future lives.

All around the ancient people saw circles, the path of the sun and moon. The winter and summer solstices and the seasons within the year. The different realms, the upper, middle and lower, formed a circle of life. Everything living had a soul, which was born and reborn repeatedly until it had learned the life lessons it needed to ascend to a higher plane.

The shaman could visit these domains in their search for knowledge and healing.

The Dagur Mongols in Inner Mongolia used the word Solongo "rainbow" for the shamans' power dreams, so the shaman may travel in his sleep over the rainbow to another world.
Shamans practise an animistic religion, meaning all humans, animals, and all things in nature have a soul or spirit with several meanings and with original characters.[11]

Nature has always been an inspiration to humanity. From the earliest times, we have depended on all living things. Whether it is animals for hunting for meat and skins or sun and rain for crops. We still find ourselves inspired and dependent on nature today. This dependence is especially true for Turkic peoples in Siberia and the Mongols. The endlessness of the steppe, the taiga[12], the forest, and the blue sky—this is the world of nature in Siberia. Lake Baikal and the mountain range of the

---

[2] Wikipedia, Paleolithic.
[3] **Error! Digit expected.**
[4] Aldo Colleoni, *Mongolian shamanism* (Italy? Ulaanbaatar: National Research Institutue ; Mongolian Academy of Sciences, 2005).
[5] Henry N. editor Michael and V. N. Chernetsan, *Studies in Siberian shamanism* ([Toronto]: Published for the Arctic Institute of North America by University of Toronto Press, 1963).
[6] https://en.wikipedia.org/wiki/Buryatia, Buryatia.
[7] Wikipedia, TibetanEmpire.
[8] Marc Petit and Christian Lequindre, *Nepal : Shamanism and tribal sculpture* ([Gollion]: Infolio, 2009).
[9] Wikipedia, Tungusiclanguages.
[10] Wikipedia, Shamanism.
[11] http://www.face-music.ch/bi_bid/historyoftengerism.html, ShamanismTengerisminMongoliainEnglish.
[12] Wikipedia, Taiga.

Altai, the Khangai, and the Sayan. This way of life is well expressed in the word tegsh, which means living your life in balance with the world of nature and human society.

The mythology of the Siberian peoples and the Mongol tales, which parents tell their children, explains the reasons things in nature are created. They explain that animals and trees have spirits and souls in the same way as human beings. The forests, mountains, lakes, rivers, and rocks also all have their spirits and souls and they need our respect for the gifts they present to humanity as foodstuff and shelter.[13]

The difference between soul and spirit is explained by only human beings having a soul; spirit is an abstract notion for a wide range of natural phenomena. The opinion is that animism must have developed from the dream experience, where people feel as if they existed independently from their bodies, flying in and to other worlds. In short, the soul takes "journeys" outside the body. During such dream journeys, they could meet dead relatives, friends, or their spirits and souls.[14]

Beliefs and practices that have been categorized as "shamanic" have attracted the interest of scholars from a wide variety of disciplines, including anthropologists, archaeologists, historians, religious studies scholars, philosophers and psychologists. Hundreds of books and academic papers on the subject have been produced, with a peer-reviewed academic journal being devoted to the study of shamanism.[15]

In the 20th century, many Westerners involved in counter-cultural movements have created modern magico-religious practices influenced by their ideas of Indigenous religions from across the world, creating what has been termed neoshamanism or the neoshamanic movement. The movement has affected the development of many neopagan practices, as well as faced a backlash and accusations of cultural appropriation, exploitation, and misrepresentation when outside observers have tried to represent cultures to which they do not belong. Although the term has been used to describe indigenous spiritual practices, some have critiqued the term shamanism as a generalizing descriptor of complex and diverse spiritual practices that are specific to different indigenous nations and tribes. Use of the term may impose simplicity on diverse and complex indigenous cultures, reinforce racist ideas, and perpetuate notions of "other" from a colonial perspective.[16]

There is no agreed-on definition of the term Shamanism. The four outstanding definitions noted by English Historian Ronald Hutton are[17]

- The first refers to "anybody who contacts a spirit world while in an altered state of consciousness."

- The second definition limits the term to refer to those who contact a spirit world while in an altered state of consciousness at the behest of others.

- The third definition attempts to distinguish shamans from other magico-religious specialists who are believed to contact spirits, such as "mediums," "witch doctors," "spiritual healers" or

---

[13] http://www.face-music.ch/bi_bid/historyoftengerism.html, ShamanismTengerisminMongoliainEnglish.
[14] http://www.face-music.ch/bi_bid/historyoftengerism.html, ShamanismTengerisminMongoliainEnglish.
[15] Wikipedia, Shamanism.
[16] Wikipedia, Shamanism.
[17] Wikipedia, Shamanism.

"prophets," by claiming that shamans undertake some particular technique not used by the others. Problematically, scholars advocating the third view have failed to agree on what the defining technique should be.

- The fourth definition identified by Hutton uses "shamanism" to refer to the Indigenous religions of Siberia and neighbouring parts of Asia[18]. According to the Golomt Center for Shamanic Studies, a Mongolian organization of shamans, the Evenk word shaman would more accurately be translated as "priest."

In this book, I agree with the first two definitions and the fourth. There are sufficiently obvious distinctions between a shaman and his or her practice in the regions mentioned earlier, and activities such as mediumship, witch doctors, or prophets.

3.1. The Shaman Calling

Shamans are distinguished from other people in that they have a shaman spirit which selects and initiates them. This spirit is known by many names, including utha[19], and an onggor among the Buryats and Dagur. An onggor is a soul spoor of previous and dead shamans. When the onggor enters the individual and becomes identified with their soul, that person has to become a shaman. Among the Buryats and Dagur. It acts like an extra soul and is a source of power and controls the shaman's encounters with other spirits, some of which may also become helper spirits. While a shaman may show a proclivity for shamanizing from an early age, the utha—I use the Buryat term for simplicity will manifest itself suddenly, resulting in mental or physical illness. During the illness, a shaman-to-be will see in which the utha will initiate him. Common elements in the vision include travel to the upper world and the dismemberment and reassembly of the shaman's body so that it will be new and empowered for his work. When the new shaman falls ill, the shaman who will examine him will recognize at once that he has been selected by an utha spirit. At that point, if he agrees to become a shaman, he can be healed; otherwise he will usually die. The training and initiation which follow his recovery are only a confirmation of the initiation which he experienced in the spirit world.[20]

In the Saami[21] traditions of Northern Europe, not just anyone can become a noaidi (shaman), only those who had special talents. The noaidi was chosen by spirits who were not of this world. The person who is chosen for this carried a heavy burden, since he or she had responsibility for the well-being of the entire siida or tribe. And that person also had to be exposed to very demanding training. During the training, he/she became familiar with and used to dealing with the spirits— noaidegázzi—who would be helpers in the practice of noaidevuohta. (Source: Solbakk, Aage. What We Believe in: Noaidevuohta—An Introduction to the Religion of the Northern Saami. Kárášjohka: ČálliidLágádus vuođđudus—Authors' Publisher Foundation, 2009, p. 15) [22]

---

[18] Wikipedia, Asia.
[19] http://buryatmongol.org/a-course-in-mongolian-shamanism/the-shaman/becoming-a-shaman/, BecomingaShaman.
[20] http://buryatmongol.org/a-course-in-mongolian-shamanism/the-shaman/becoming-a-shaman/, BecomingaShaman.
[21] Wikipedia, Samipeople.
[22] https://www.facebook.com/EuropeShamanism/photos/a.186820488859769/560852338123247/?type=3, HennoEriksonParks-Posts.

4. Tngri, Tengri

The Tengri religion has been recorded in Chinese chronicles from the fourth century BC onwards. Tngri was the sky god and prevailing religion of the Xiongnu, Bulgars, Huns, and possibly the Manus and Magyars people.[23] It was also the state religion of several medieval states: as: Göktürk Khaganate, Western Turkic Khaganate, Eastern Turkic Khaganate, Old Great Bulgaria, Danube Bulgaria, Volga Bulgaria, and Eastern Tourkia (Khazaria).[24]

In Tengriism, the meaning of life is found in living in harmony with the natural universe. Tengriist believers view their existence as sustained by the celestial blue sky, Tengri, the fertile Mother-Earth, and life-spirit Eje. Heaven, Earth, the spirits of nature and ancestors provide for every need and protect all humans. By living an upright and respectful life, a human being will keep his world in balance and experience prosperity, well-being, and success. Shamans play an important role in restoring balance when a disaster or illness occurs.[25]

In the pantheon of Mongolian shamanism, Tngri, Tengri, or tegri make up the highest class of divinities.
Different references describe various chief deities. The deities are divided into groups which included black and terrifying, and white or benevolent, as well as based on the points of the compass.[26]

The clan-based Mongolian society is based on a complex spiritual hierarchy.[27] They are attested to in the oldest written source in Mongolian, The Secret History of the Mongols.[28][29] The highest deity, Tngri, is the "supreme god of heaven" and is derived from, the primary chief deity in the religion of the early Turkic[30] and Mongolic[31] peoples, and also goes by Möngke Tngri ("Eternal Heaven") or Erketü Tngri ("Mighty Heaven"); he rules the 99 Tngri as Köke Möngke Tngri ("Blue Eternal Heaven").[32]

Several further divisions are possible. The Tngri comprises groups including the gods of the four corners, five wind gods, five gods of the entrance and five of the door, five of the horizontal, plus many more.[33]

At the top of the hierarchy are 99 Tngri of which 55 are "white," or benevolent, and 44 are terrifying or "black"; There are 77 natigais or "earth mothers" plus several others. The Tngri was called upon only by leaders and great shamans and were common to all the clans. Black Tngri was invoked only by black shamans "against evil from outside and for securing victory in war."[34]

<u>Other Souls and Spirits included…</u>

---

[23] Wikipedia, Xiongnu.
[24] Wikipedia, Tengrism.
[25] https://www.newworldencyclopedia.org/entry/Tengriism, TengriismNewWorldEncyclopedia.
[26] Wikipedia, Tngri.
[27] Wikipedia, Tngri.
[28] Wikipedia, TheSecretHistoryoftheMongols.
[29] , (!!! INVALID CITATION !!!).
[30] Wikipedia, Turkiclanguages.
[31] Wikipedia, Mongols.
[32] Wikipedia, Tngri.
[33] Wikipedia, Tngri.
[34] Wikipedia, Tngri.

- Souls of the Great Shamans: Protector-Spirits of the Clan
- Souls of the Simple Shamans: Guardian-Spirits of Localities
- The Three Spirits Accepting Supplication

<u>Division of the gods and spirits of Mongol shamanism:</u>

- White and Black deities
- Lord-Spirits of the clan
- Protector-Spirits of the clan
- Guardian-Spirits of the clan
- White Spirits of Nobles of the clan
- Black Spirits of Commoners of the clan
- Evil Spirits

Associated with Tengri is another chief deity, Qormusata Tngri, described by one scholar as the more active being and compared to the Hindu[35] god of heaven Indra[36]. Besides the 99 Tngri, there are also "seventy-seven levels of Mother Earth" and 33 other gods; the latter, like the Tngri, are ruled by Qormusata Tngri.[37]

Tngri is invoked only by the highest shamans and leaders for special occasions; they continue to be venerated, especially in black shamanism. Chief among the Tngri is Qormusata Tngri and Mongke [Khan] Tngri.[38]

The Tengriist universe comprised three worlds:
- A lower or underground world,
- the middle world in which human beings lived,
- the upper spiritual world.

---

[35] Wikipedia, Hinduism.
[36] Wikipedia, Indra.
[37] Wikipedia, Tngri.
[38] Wikipedia, Tngri.

Figure 1. Tree of Life. Image by Dmytro from Pixabay

The lower world could be entered by a spiritual "river." The middle world is connected with the upper world by a sacred World Tree. There are no official symbols of Tengriism. However, the symbol of the World Tree with nine levels and four directions is common. Rituals and ceremonies were typically performed on a mountaintop or by a sacred tree, places where human beings could come into contact with the spiritual world.[39]

The ancient Turks perceived Yer—Earth and Tengri—Spirit of the Sky as two complimentary aspects of a single beginning. Tengri was unknown. He was not visualized as a person, although

---

[39] https://www.newworldencyclopedia.org/entry/Tengriism, TengriismNewWorldEncyclopedia.

he was said to have at least two sons. Tengri was considered being timeless and infinite, like a blue sky.

A man was born and lived in a material shell on the earth, distinct from other men; he was given a Kut—soul at birth by Tengri, who took it back when he died. Tengri was considered a father, Yer a mother. Tengri was supreme, and any supplication to Yer also included the name of Tengri.[40]

For the ancient Turks and Mongols, Tengri governed all existence on earth, determining the fate of individuals and that of entire nations and their rulers. Tengri was believed to act of his own volition, but with fairness, meting out rewards and punishments. It was believed that Tengri assisted those who revered him and who were active in trying to accomplish his will.

The term Kuk-Tengri—Blue Sky referred to a spiritual, celestial "sky," and the epithet "Kuk" (blue), when applied to an animal, such as a horse (Kuk at), ram (kuk teke), bull (kuk ugez), or deer (kuk bolan), was a reference to the animal's divine origin.

Tengri was omnipresent and was worshiped simply by lifting hands upwards and bowing low, praying for him to give a good mind and health, and to help perform good deeds.
In Irk Bitig[41], Tengri is mentioned as Türük Tängrisi—God of Turks. According to many academics, at the imperial level, especially by the 12th—13th centuries, Tengrism was a monotheistic religion; most contemporary Tengrists still presents it as being monotheistic today.

Tengri differs from Siberian shamanism in that the people in power practising it were not small bands of hunter-gatherers like the Paleosiberians but a continuous succession of pastoral, semi-sedentarized khanates[42] and empires from the Xiongnu (founded 209 B.C.) to the Mongol Empire (13th century).[43]

Tengri developed in the eastern steppes and enjoyed more centralized and hierarchical forms of government than in the western steppe. It is more centralized and less polytheistic, less mythical—intensive and more historically focused than the paganism that grew out of the western Proto-Indo-European religion. Nonetheless, the chief god Tengri ("Heaven") is considered strikingly similar to the Indo-European sky god *Dyeus, and the structure of the reconstructed Proto-Indo-European religion is closer to that of the early Turks than to the religion of any people of Near Eastern or Mediterranean antiquity.[44]

Archaeological research has revealed that the Magyar people, today known as Hungarians, worshiped Tengri until the arrival of Christianity into the 10th century.

Today Tengrism continues to exist in the distant Turko-Mongolian regions of Russia.

---

[40] https://www.newworldencyclopedia.org/entry/Tengriism, TengriismNewWorldEncyclopedia.
[41] Wikipedia, IrkBitig.
[42] Wikipedia, Khanate.
[43] Wikipedia, Tengrism.
[44] Wikipedia, Tengrism.

Genghis Khan and several generations of his followers were Tengrian believers and "Shaman-Kings" until his fifth-generation descendant, Uzbeg Khan, turned to Islam in the 14th century. Old Tengrist prayers have come down to us from the Secret History of the Mongols[45] [46] (13th century).

4.1. Tengri Shamanism

Shamans and Shamanesses encompassed all that is Tengri and the world order, as they saw it in their animistic belief that there is energy in all things, even plants, animals, and inanimate objects.

Tengrist Shamanism[47] includes additional spirits and gods to be worshiped and visited during healing sessions.

- Umay: goddess of fertility, and often associated with the earth-mother goddesses. The word "Umay" comes from the Mongolian "Umai," which means "womb." Umay, the goddess, is the protector of children and mothers.

- Bai-Ulgen: the deity of creation. And the next most worshiped deity after Tengri. He is the god with no end and no beginning. Therefore, he always existed and never stopped being. His name comes from Turkic Bay (rich) and Ulgen (magnificent). He lives in the sky above the stars, moon, and sun. Bai-Ulgen is the protector of humankind against the evil deity Erlik.

- Ulgen is the other son of Bai-Ulgen and is the ruler of the upper world.

- Erklig: The powerful god of Space. He moves the stars, moons, planets, and all the cosmic objects. In Tengri Shamanism, Erklig is also the master of the planet Venus. Tengri beliefs sustain that the falling stars are the hot arrows of Erklig.

- Erlik: The evil deity of the underworld. He is also the deity of death. Erlik is the first deity created by Bai-Ulgen. Erlik is known as the son of Bai-Ulgen. But Erlik became full of pride. And his actions led to his banishment to the underworld or hell. Erlik was also present at the creation of humanity. He teaches humanity how to sin. Shamans often describe him as a monster with human body but the face and teeth of a pig.

- Erlik is associated with disasters and epidemics among people or cattle, which he caused so that man would be forced to offer him a sacrifice. People were afraid to say his name, and called him Kara-Name (something black) instead. Erlik had sons who helped him to rule the underground world, where there were lakes, rivers and seas. His daughters, numbering from two to nine in Turkic myths, were described as idle, sexually promiscuous, temptresses. Erlik was thought to associate closely with shamans. He rarely caused evil to man, and did not control peoples' souls but evil spirits from his domain would ascend to the physical road and do harm. Sacrifices were always conducted at night.

---

[45] Wikipedia, TheSecretHistoryoftheMongols.
[46] .
[47] https://spiritualgrowthguide.com/tengri-shamanism/, TengriShamanism-TheDeitiesOfTengrism-SpiritualGrowthGuide.

5. Contemporary Tengrism

New Tengrism is a fairly "new" term. It is not an extension of Tengri, as the Mongols and Turkic tribes on the steppes knew it when Genghis Khan ruled.

The spelling "Tengrism" for the religion of the ancient Turks is found in the works of the 19th century Kazakh Russophone ethnographer Shoqan Walikhanov. The term was introduced into a wide scientific circulation in 1956 by Jean-Paul Roux and later in the 1960s as a term of English-language papers.

A revival of Tengrism has played a role in the search for native spiritual roots and Pan-Turkism ideology since the 1990s, especially, in Kyrgyzstan, Kazakhstan, Mongolia, some autonomous republics of the Russian Federation (Tatarstan, Bashkortostan, Buryatia, Yakutia, and others), among the Crimean Karaites and Crimean Tatars.[48]

After the 1908 Young Turk Revolution[49], in what was the Ottoman Empire and especially the proclamation of the Republic in 1923, a nationalist ideology of Turanism and Kemalism contributed to the revival of Tengrism. Islamic censorship was abolished, which allowed an objective study of the pre-Islamic religion of the Turks. The Turkish language was purified of Arabic, Persian, and other borrowings. A number of figures, if they did not officially abandon Islam, but adopted Turkic names, such as Mustafa Kemal Atatürk[50] — "father of Turks" i.e., President on Modern Turkey 1923–1958, and the historian of religion and ideologist of the Kemalist regime Ziya Gökalp (Gökalp — "sky hero"). [51]

Tengrism has been advocated in intellectual circles of the Turkic nations of Central Asia (Kyrgyzstan with Kazakhstan) and Russia, Tatarstan and Bashkortostan since the dissolution of the Soviet Union during the 1990s. Still practised, it is undergoing an organized revival in Buryatia, Sakha (Yakutia), Khakassia, Tuva and other Turkic nations in Siberia. Altaian Burkhanism and Chuvash Vattisen Yaly are movements similar to Tengrism.

Tengrism has very few active adherents - 1990s, but its revival of an ethnic religion reached a larger audience in intellectual circles. Former presidents of Kazakhstan Nursultan Nazarbayev and Kyrgyzstani Askar Akayev have called Tengrism the national, "natural" religion of the Turkic peoples. So, during the 2002 trip to Khakassia, Russia, Akayev spoke out that a visit to the Yenisei River and the runic steles constituted "a pilgrimage to a holy place for the Kyrgyz" just like the pilgrimage to Mecca. Presenting Islam as foreign to the Turkic peoples and as Semitic religion together with Christianity and Judaism, adherents are found primarily among the nationalistic parties of Central Asia. Tengrism may be interpreted as a Turkic version of Russian neopaganism, which is already well established. It is partly similar to the new religious movements, such as New Age.[52] [53] [54]

---

[48] Wikipedia, Tengrism.
[49] Feroz Ahmad, "The Young Turk Revolution," *Journal of Contemporary History* 3, no. 3 (2016), https://doi.org/10.1177/002200946800300302.
[50] Wikipedia, MustafaKemalAtatürk.
[51] Wikipedia, Tengrism.
[52] Merriam-Webster, DefinitionofNewAge.
[53] Wikipedia, NewAge.
[54] Wikipedia, Tengrism.

6. Ancestor Worship

The veneration of the dead, including one's ancestors, is based on love and respect for the deceased.[55]

In some cultures, ancestor worship is related to beliefs that the dead have a continued existence, and may possess the ability to influence the fortune of the living. Ancestors are seen as being able to intercede on behalf of the living, often as messengers between humans and God. To this end, religions, such as the Eastern Orthodox and Roman Catholic Churches, venerate saints as intercessors with God; the latter also believes in prayer for departed souls in Purgatory. Other religious groups, however, consider veneration of the dead to be idolatry and a sin.[56]

Ancestors were once living beings. As a young child, I can recall sitting in my grandmother's wonderful old arm chair when she was not around, I could touch her and watch her as she cooked. She knew what I was thinking, and sometimes I knew what she thought of me and how earnest was my upbringing.

As an ancestor spirt, she is able to understand the challenges and successes of my life. While some cultures would say her spirit, and those of my parents, are there not for me to ask for favours but to do one's family duty. Others believe that their ancestors need to be provided for by their descendants, and their practices include offerings of food and other provisions. While still others do not believe their ancestors are aware of what their descendants do for them, but that the expression of filial piety is what is important.

Most cultures who practise ancestor veneration do not call it "ancestor worship" because of the word "worship." We go to church to worship, God, Jesus Christ, or Mary Magdalene, a saint or a miraculous event. Linking this form of belief to our ancestors seems strange or wrong because in the west, they are not considered to have become deities when they die.

Ancestor worship as an expression of family loyalty rather than deity worship and can be seen in simple things, such as visiting a deceased relative's grave, laying flowers on a grave, praying for them on their birthday or just simply finding some time to think about them on Mother's Day or Father's Day.

Rather, the act is a way to express family duty, devotion and respect and look after ancestors in their afterlives as well as seek their guidance for their living descendants. In this regard, many cultures and religions have similar practices. Generally excluded from this are rites for the dead having no specific reference to kinsmen, and beliefs about the dead in general lack any special reference to kinship.
Asking your parents, "what would you do?" When faced with a problem, it could be seen as ancestor worship because we are asking for their help and guidance to sort out a difficulty we have.

"Veneration of Ancestors" to those with a Western European Christian tradition, feels more appropriate but it does not completely convey an accurate sense of what practitioners such as the Chinese and other Buddhist and Confucian-influenced societies, as well as the African and European cultures, see themselves as doing. Their actions are consistent with the meaning of the

---

[55] Wikipedia, Venerationofthedead.
[56] Wikipedia, Venerationofthedead.

word veneration in English, which is great respect or reverence caused by the dignity, wisdom, or dedication of a person.[57]

Ancestor worship is often viewed as a religious practice rather than a religion, as there is seldom a priesthood attached to it and there is nor formal doctrine. In most cases, ancestor worship is not the only religious practice of a society; rather, it exists as part of a more comprehensive religious system.

Death rites, including funerary and mortuary rituals, are regarded as falling within the purview of ancestor worship only when memorial rights beyond the period of death and disposition of the corpse are carried out as a regular function of a kinship group.[58]

The earliest evidence of ancestor worship in China dates to the Yangshao society, which existed in the Shaanxi Provincial area before spreading to parts of northern and central China during the Neolithic period - 6000 to 1000 BCE. During the Shang dynasty, 1600 - 1046 BCE, the ancestors of the royal family were thought to reside in heaven within the feudal hierarchy of other spirit gods.

These ancestors, it was believed, could be contacted via a shaman. The shaman may assist in communing with ancestors on behalf of living family members but it is the descendant alone that shall address his/her own forefathers to intercede in the resolution of family or individual conflict.

A shaman engaged in a healing ritual may contact the clients' ancestors seeking help and advice in the cause and solution of the illness. The shaman may also negotiate with an ancestor who is upset about the actions of their living relative[s] and is causing illness or problems as a "punishment" or way to express their anger.

Advice received by the shaman from an ancestor may take them to another sprit or location in the realm they are visiting. Therefore, ancestor spirits are one form of spirit the shaman encounters when searching for answers to questions and to perform healing.

---

[57] Wikipedia, Venerationofthedead.
[58] https://www.encyclopedia.com/environment/encyclopedias-almanacs-transcripts-and-maps/ancestors-ancestor-worship, AncestorsAncestorWorship.com.

7. Shaman

Although Westerners often use the generic term "shaman" to describe all the tribal magical practitioners of Siberia and Mongolia, in practice they were divided into several different types, categories, or classes with specific magical duties and responsibilities. Using English terminology, these included "conjurors" who summoned and controlled spirits, prophets, or psychics who foresaw the future, sorcerers who practised "black magic," trance workers who travelled in spirit form to the Otherworld, healers who were experts in folk medicine and herbalism, and guides to the dead who laid out corpses and conducted funeral rites.[59]

In reality, Shame is very spiritual people in addition to their other roles as healers, bone setters, midwives, and advisors.

- Bone Setter. As the description implies, their role is focused on setting bones and resolving dislocations. They also work with back pain, bowls, sores, and other skin diseases. It is often said that a bone setter can see a broken bone as well as an imaging device.

- Midwife. The Shaman midwife inherited her power from the maternal line of familial descent. As well as ensuring that babies entered this world safely in a physical sense, she was also responsible for their spiritual protection from evil influences during birth and their well-being as children. In this sense, she took on the role of a human fairy godmother. Immediately after birth, the shaman-midwife cut the umbilical cord and then purified the newborn baby with salt water and fire. Any (female only) witnesses to the birth could only be present if they had first been ritually purified by the midwife with fire and water. During the first few weeks of a baby's life, it was very important that the proper rituals were performed to protect the child until its spirit was fully established in the material world. If they were not performed properly, then the baby's spirit might return from whence it had come. These essential rites were the responsibility of the shaman midwife and her assistants.[60]

- Shaman Smith. One of the most important and respected types of magical practitioners was the shaman Smith. In all cultures all over the world, from Europe to Africa, the Smith took a central role in tribal society and was regarded as a powerful magician or sorcerer because of his mastery over fire and skill in working with metal. In Siberia the shaman smiths made and magically consecrated the ritual metal objects used by other shamans. They were only chosen by the spirits and instead of a drum, they used their anvils to communicate with the spiritual realm. Healer and Guide. [61]

- Shaman Assistant. The role has various duties, ranging from warming the drums by the fire, over helping with the equipment up to drumming, which constitute some of the most common duties. Shamanic assistants are usually people who are very spiritual but have

---

[59] https://www.newdawnmagazine.com/articles/secrets-of-siberian-shamanism, SecretsofSiberianShamanism.
[60] https://www.newdawnmagazine.com/articles/secrets-of-siberian-shamanism, SecretsofSiberianShamanism.
[61] https://www.newdawnmagazine.com/articles/secrets-of-siberian-shamanism, SecretsofSiberianShamanism.

never had a specific calling. They do not wear specialized regalia, but often the shaman they work with will give them a protective talisman as a gift.[62]

7.1. Healer and Guide

The shaman is a healer. This is their principal role in the tribe and the community.

They have access to, and influence in, the world of benevolent and malevolent spirits, who typically enter into a trance state during a ritual, and practices divination and healing.

Soul journeying to understand what and why a person was ill and journeying to spirits that will help return health to the physical person is their primary and most essential role.

Mongol shamanism had ninety-nine deities:

- Fifty-five of these deities were White, i.e., Beneficent to mankind.
- Forty-four were Black, i.e., Terrible to all the evildoers of mankind and to the enemies of the Mongol Nation.

In total, they are the national gods of Mongol Shamanism. No commoner of any Mongol clan dared embarrass them with his insubstantial bagatelle, since they were the Spirits of Ancestors of every clan, the souls of dead chieftains, shamans, and shamanesses who during their life had devoted themselves to satisfying the requirements of the members of clans and who in the World of Spirits should solve the difficulties in the life of the members of their clans, commoners, and nobles and even serfs.

Minor spirits of a clan's ancestors were divided into several classes. The largest among them were the class of the souls of the clans' chieftains, introduced after their death by a special solemn shamanist right to the communion of Clan Ancestors and thus becoming members of the communion and of the Benevolent Lord-Spirits who played a very important role in the life of a clan and its members.

Black shamanism is a kind of shamanism practised in Mongolia and Siberia. It is specifically opposed to yellow shamanism, which incorporates rituals and traditions from Buddhism. Black Shamans are usually perceived as working with evil spirits, while white Shamans with spirits of the upper world.

Other Souls and Spirits included…

- Souls of the Great Shamans: Protector-Spirits of the Clan
- Souls of the Simple Shamans: Guardian-Spirits of Localities
- The Three Spirits Accepting Supplication

<u>Division of the gods and spirits of Mongol shamanism:</u>

White and Black deities

---

[62] http://www.face-music.ch/bi_bid/historyoftengerism.html, ShamanismTengerisminMongoliainEnglish.

> Lord-Spirits of the clan
> Protector-Spirits of the clan
> Guardian-Spirits of the clan
> White Spirits of Nobles of the clan
> Black Spirits of Commoners of the clan
> Evil Spirits

Chinggis Khan, or Genghis Khan, the renowned Mongolian leader, practised Black Shamanism, though he himself was not a shaman.

The banner at the head of the Mongol Armies that subjugated China and got as far as eastern Europe was black. But this should not be confused with Chinggis Khan and his practice of Black Shamanism. A tribe would have black and white banners in the centre of their camp.

The banners were each guarded together with white and black Lord Spirits of the Clan. Nobles of the clan would escort the banners during ceremonies and feasts.

In battle, the black banner was believed to bring victory over Mongol enemies, while the white banner remained in camp.

7.2. Oracle

Shaman were astrologers and oracles. Everyone, especially tribal leaders, wants to know what the future will bring. Will it bring war, will they be successful in the struggle? Will crops and animal husbandry be successful? Will the tribe merge with another through marriage?

The history of the shaman in this role goes back into the very remote past, before the advent of Buddhism in Tibet in the seventh century.

Historically, this Oracle, divination and Astrology were a feature of Bon in pre-Buddhist Tibet. The Bon cosmology was divided into three worlds.

- The upper world of the gods.
- An intermediate world of spirits, of subtle beings.
- The solid or physical world we know as the earth.

Bon also held the spirit or soul of the individual, which was a world or realm of energy which humans are able to contact. For example, humans are able to connect with physical things, such as food, a chair, and other people. On the spiritual level, they are able to connect at the psychic level with other spirits and those on the different levels, such as the first and second.

When Buddhists brought Buddhist Dharma to Tibet, they were able to include the Bon world view on their own because Buddhism holds the view. The Buddhist world exists in three parts: one solid, one psychic and one mental.

The change happened when the famous Tantric master Guru Padmasambhava came to Tibet and tamed the subtle world—the deities of the Bonpos—and bound them under oath to obey and defend the Buddhist teaching. He made these powers, which we can call deities, protectors of the Buddhist faith and of Buddhist practitioners. They became Cho sung, protectors of the Dharma. According to Tibetan tradition, he tamed these beings through the powerful invocation of mantras and powerful spells, which bound them to obey those who held the power of these spells. Guru Padmasambhava tamed these beings. He made them protectors of the Dharma and obliged or convinced them to help practitioners of Buddha Dharma by communicating, giving advice, foretelling the future and even healing people.

The deities are sentient beings. They are beings, just like people or animals and anyone else, but without a body. They also have a mind or spirit, and a voice. Without a body, they cannot communicate with those who communicate on a bodily level. So, they are samsaric beings.

Samsara is the term for the everlasting cycle of being. It is the cycle of becoming and passing away, or the cycle of rebirths in the Indian religions of Hinduism, Buddhism and Jainism.

As such, they are not higher gods, as we would understand the great gods of India or Tibet. They are gods linked to the land, mountains, lakes and to the geographical features. We could in a way that mountains and lakes are their bodily aspect. So, they are the subtle aspect: the speech and mind aspect of mountains, valleys, rivers, and lakes, especially mountains and lakes.

7.1. Continuity

They were the spiritual leader of a group or tribe. The belief and practice of Shamanism incorporate a range of beliefs, customs, ceremonies, and rituals regarding communication with the spiritual world in which their religious leader, the Shaman, enters supernatural realms, particularly when the tribe is facing adversity or needs to obtain solutions to problems afflicting the community, including sickness.

They provided continuity to the tribe and a reliable connection to the spirit world. In this way, they were a communicator from the human physical world to the spirit world and back again.
They were an educator of people about the spirit world as well as about medicines and herbs and natural healing solutions. They kept the tribal stories, myths, and essential tribal wisdom that made the tribe they belonged to different from another.

They understood and passed down understanding of trance states, how to induce them and how to control them. Their clothing, symbolic regalia and objects were passed down to enrich subsequent generations of shamans.

They are the keepers of tradition, ancient texts, books, and scripts as well as the way things should be done. Songs, dances, music, and observance are also carried forward from the shaman to shamans within the tribe.

Shamans usually have expert knowledge of medicinal plants native to their area, and an herbal treatment is often prescribed. It is believed shamans learn directly from the plants, harnessing their effects and healing properties, after obtaining permission from the indwelling or patron spirits.

The chieftains and nobles may change, but the shaman remains.

7.2. Protector

One of a shaman's main functions is to protect individuals from hostile supernatural influences.

The shaman may act as a psychopomp conducting the spirits of individuals who have just died to the proper refuge for dead spirits.

Psychopomp literally means "guide of souls") are creatures, spirits, angels, or deities in many religions whose responsibility is to escort newly deceased souls from Earth to the afterlife. They do not judge the deceased, but simply guide them. Appearing frequently on funerary art, psychopomps have been depicted at different times and in different cultures as anthropomorphic entities, horses, deer, dogs, whip-poor-wills, ravens, crows, vultures, owls, sparrows and cuckoos. When seen as birds, they are often seen in huge masses, waiting outside the home of the dying.

7.3. Other Traditions of Shaman Selection

Banjhakri [63] and Banjhākrini[64] are shamanic deities in the tradition of the Kirati people of Nepal[65]. They are a couple, and possibly different aspects of the same being. They are supernatural shamans of the forest. In the Nepali language, ban means "wilderness," jhākri means "shaman," and Jhākrini means "shamaness." Banjhākrini is also known as Lemlemey.

Banjhākri is a short, wild, simian trickster who is a descendant of the Sun. His ears are large and his feet point backward. Long, matted hair covers his entire body, except for his face and palms, and he plays a golden dhyāngro. The dhyangro is the frame drum played by Nepali jhākri.

Banjhākri finds human children who have the potential to be great shamans, and takes them back to his cave for training.

The abductee is taught about the forest, spirits, life, death and healing. Taught in this way, when the abductee was returned to their home, their village and their community after a few days, they were more powerful than any shaman taught by a human. They are prototypical models for becoming a shaman in Nepal and, so to speak, a mark of distinction and an epithet of supernatural potency and unofficial status. The abductee may be taken again for further training. The Banjhākri may also appear in dreams to continue teaching.

If the abductees were found to have physical problems, scars, or not pure of heart, or if they failed the initiation ceremony at the end of their stay, or had been disobedient, they would be thrown out of the Banjhakri camp and ran the risk of being captured by his ferocious and cannibalistic mate, the Banjhakrini who would kill them with her gold cycle and eat their bodies.

In all the stories about the Banjhakri, they are the teacher, the guide, the instructor, the leader and the mentor, but now he wants to learn. They teach using a combination of telepathy and a secret language the initiate learns.

Like the yeti, Banjhakri and Banjhakrini can be seen in our world, and not just in the spirit world. However, only powerful shamans can see them. Although both Banjhakri and yeti are apelike, yeti is taller than humans, whereas Banjhakri is only about 1–1.5 metres (3–5 feet) tall. Both have fur covering their entire body except for their hands and their face. Their feet face backwards. This

---

[63] Wikipedia, BanjhakriandBanjhakrini.
[64] Wikipedia, BanjhakriandBanjhakrini.

means if tracks are found, the trackers are inevitably going in the wrong direction if they follow the impressions believing them to be normal human feet. The yeti lives in the high mountain pass and are teachers of yogi and others that seek the peace and energy of high mountains and live there, in caves.

The Banjhakri are the master of Liminality. They stand at the juncture of two realities, in between categories and boundaries. They are physical and spiritual. Human and animal, beings of dreams and of reality. They are the masters in a numinous unbounded space where everything is backwards, opposite, and dangerous. They are the neophytes' guides through the dark night before initiatory rebirth.

We are used to seeing and thinking of shamans in their traditional cultures. But there is shaman alive and well today and they walk, talk, and dress in the ways that fit in completely with the societies in which they live.

A person visiting a traditional shaman in a traditional culture may not think twice about a shaman dressing in a bear skin to call on and work with a helping spirit who happens to be a bear. In modern western culture, that would not be acceptable. A modern shaman may wear a bear claw on a chain or cord under their shirt instead. The claw would not be seen by anyone present but the effect would be the same during the ceremony. And there is a shaman who has such a relationship with their helping spirits that even a bear claw is not required.

A few years ago I developed intense pain in my back and had difficulty breathing. An ambulance took me to the hospital, where I spent the rest for the day and a night in the Emergency Room. Lying on the bed, surrounded by curtains, I could only hear the voices and words of the other patients, doctors, and nurses. There was nothing to see; it seemed as if they were from another world.

In the spaces next to me, patients would come and go. The space next to me suddenly was filled with violent words spoken with terrible energy and the sounds of metal restraints jangling against the fastening points of the bed. The patient had been strapped and chained to their bed; they were confined and in pain, I heard it all. It went on for hours. Finally, the diagnosis was that a family doctor had changed the calming meditation prescribed by the hospital and the change was not a good change.

After a few hours on different medications, the patient was quietened and they disappeared to somewhere else in the hospital and special cleaning staff arrived to wipe down and sanitize the space the patient had occupied.

Then in the distance, the sound of a caring relative to an elderly relative, their father, whom they loved very much. Whatever the cause, the elderly relative had been fitted with a diaper and the advice was to use it, but he resisted. Throughout his life, he had been brought not to lie there and pee, instead to use a toilet. The caring relative calmly and repeatedly affirmed that now was different, life was different and so was their existence.

Then, a small break in the curtains. I could see out. I could see an elderly man and his relatives. He had just arrived and seemed to be quite lively, but as the hours passed, the life essence of him drained away. At the point I left the ER, he was unresponsive and several conferences with doctors had come and gone. Now that I look at it, his soul was ready to leave, but his physical container, his body was still holding on with its autonomic processes.

I have always been aware of my guides, one in particular, she has looked after and helped me many times and we have a strong relationship.

At 1 a.m. a "white alert" was announced over the intercom. Sounds of screaming, swearing, and smashing of equipment and doors banging raged through the ER. A patient with a mental disorder had managed to side step their attendant and was roaming the ER. The sounds would be distant one moment and almost next to my small curtained space the next. It seemed to be a soul in torment, tormented by dark energy that would eventually destroy the physical container.

I called on my guides and with all my heart affirmed by adherence to "being a soul, a spirit of light, and love," today I would say I am a white shaman. As I affirmed my intention over and over again, the tortured voice became more distant, and was gone.

A flurry of activity with doctors followed. They had diagnosed a blood clot on the back of one of my lungs. I was released several hours later with a course of medication and follow-up tests to be done.

It was a month or so after this experience that a new guide appeared: a Tibetan White Shaman. She had been born in AD 521; she would lead me through the induction as a White Shaman, and together with my Reiki guides would provide shamanic energy and experience to healing sessions.

A very modern, shamanic initiation crisis, which differs from traditional initiatory crisis of the future shaman is usually indicated by involuntary shaking, induced by the Spirits in some form or other. This state is also called the "shamanic illness." The shamanistic initiatory crisis functions as an—involuntary—rite of passage for the future shaman, and it involves both a more-or-less serious physical illness and/or a psychological crisis. This state is well attested across all shamanic regions. Next to illness, the shaman-to-be may be struck by lightning and may dream of thunder, or may have a near-death experience.

8. Soul

The word "soul" can refer to the Spirit of God. Or, if the person speaking to me does not want to refer to "God," just "Spirit." It exists in each individual; it is an ever-existing, ever-conscious, ever-new bliss.

Identification of Soul with the physical body becomes the nature of the individual. References to "spiritual progress" or "soul evolution" use this definition, because the soul that is aware of its true identity as part of God is already perfect. Souls only evolve or progress in the sense that they go from identifying with their physical bodies to identifying with God. This can also be called the ego.

8.1. Dictionary Definition

- The physical structure and material substance of an animal or plant, living or dead [66]

Merriam Webster Dictionary[67]

- the immaterial essence, animating principle, or actuating cause of an individual life
- the spiritual principle embodied in human beings, all rational and spiritual beings, or the universe
- Capitalized, Christian Science: GOD senses
- a person's total self
- an active or essential part
- of a moving spirit: LEADER
- the moral and emotional nature of human beings
- the quality that arouses emotion and sentiment
- spiritual or moral force: FERVOUR

8.2. Etymology

In Modern English, the word "soul" is derived from Old English sáwol, sáwel, was first attested in the 8th century poem Beowulf v. 2820 and in the Vespasian Psalter 77.50. It is cognate with other German and Baltic terms for the same idea, including Gothic saiwala, Old High German sêula, sêla, Old Saxon sêola, Old Low Franconian sêla, sîla, Old Norse sála, and Lithuanian siela. Deeper etymology of the Germanic word is unclear.[68]

---

[66] Dictionary.com, DefinitionofBodyatDictionary.com.
[67] Merriam-Webster Dictionary, DefinitionofSoulbyMerriam-Webster.
[68] Wikipedia, Soul.

The original concept behind the Germanic root is thought to mean "coming from or belonging to the sea (or lake)," because of the Germanic and pre-Celtic belief in souls emerging from and returning to sacred lakes, Old Saxon sêola (soul) compared to Old Saxon sêo (sea). [69]

In the Tibetan world view, there is no destructive death at the end of life as it is in the west. Instead, there is reincarnation, rebirth, and a transition into a new life. What we do in this life, the good and bad deeds, or Karma influence the rebirth of our soul and how it will continue to seek enlightenment.

The soul[70] in many religious, philosophical, and mythological traditions is the incorporeal[71] essence, the nonmaterial form of a living being. Soul or psyche (comprises the mental abilities of a living being: reason, character, feeling, consciousness, memory, perception, thinking, etc. Depending on the philosophical system, a soul may be mortal or immortal.

8.3. Incorporeal Essence

The soul includes other forms of incorporeal essence; it includes our emotions, our will to do something, or not. Our thoughts and our feelings. It is through our soul that we sense hurt and suffering as well as pleasure and enjoyment. Our soul experiences the energy and drive, or discouragement of external stimulus and how we respond to it.

When we collect all these incorporeal reactions to stimulus, we come to life and others around is, human or animal react to us. Some people have good relations with other humans and animals; some do not. This outward expression of the soul becomes what we and others describe as our personality.

To a great extent, the expression of our personality is reinforced by repeated, similar reactions from those around us. External shocks and changes can change our personality. Sudden, unforeseen loss of a loved one, human or animal can be so fundamental that other aspects of our soul come to the surface that had previously not had expression.

8.4. Human Body

The human body is the material and physical structure of a human being. It is composed of many different types of cells that together create tissues and subsequently organ systems. They ensure homeostasis and the viability of the human body. [72]

It comprises a head, neck, trunk (which includes the thorax and abdomen), arms and hands, legs and feet. [73]

The study of the human body involves anatomy, physiology, histology, and embryology. The body varies anatomically in known ways. Physiology focuses on the systems and organs of the human

---

[69] Wikipedia, Soul.
[70] Wikipedia, Soul.
[71] Dictionary.com, Incorporeal.
[72] Wikipedia, Humanbody.
[73] Wikipedia, Humanbody.

body and their functions. Many systems and mechanisms interact in order to maintain homeostasis, with safe levels of substances such as sugar and oxygen in the blood. [74]

The body is studied by health professionals, physiologists, anatomists, and by artists to assist them in their work.[75]

It is the physical entity we interact with, on the subway, in the grocery store, at work, in love or when we are in conflict.

The physical body is what we find attractive in a man or woman until we know the person better. It is the physical body that creates limitations, such being confined to a wheelchair, and it grants gifts, such as being artistic or proficient and admired in sports. All of these gifts and limitations are part of the boundary to the learning experience of the soul and in which the spirit must work.

8.5. Other Bodies

Human beings are not the only physical beings that have a body; animals, plants, and cells also have bodies.

Animals are multicellular eukaryotic organisms that from the biological kingdom Animalia. With few exceptions, animals consume organic material, breathe oxygen, are able to move, can reproduce sexually, and grow from a hollow sphere of cells, the blastula, during embryonic development. Over 1.5 million living animal species have been described—of which around 1 million are insects—but it has been estimated there are over 7 million animal species in total. Animals range in length from 8.5 millionths of a meter to 33.6 metres (110 ft). They have complex interactions with each other and their environments, forming intricate food webs. The kingdom Animalia includes humans, but in colloquial use the term animal often refers only to non-human animals. The scientific study of animals is known as zoology.[76]

When we consider the cellular world, cellular respiration[77] is a guide as to the activity in the cell and the world within and without the cell and the life process taking place in it, which is a mirror of what is taking place in human and animal bodies.

The body is a complex organization of cells, bones, and connective tissues, which when taken together inhabit physical space, whether alive or dead, even when cremated, the body ashes take up space. If you reach out with your index finger, you can touch your body and that of other human beings as well as animals and you can use tools such as microscopes to study other life forms.

8.6. Spirit

What we call a Spirit[78][79][80] is also incorporeal. If the soul exists within us and gathers experience through lifetime after lifetime, then in each life it is the spirit that gives expression to the soul's

---

[74] Wikipedia, Humanbody.
[75] Wikipedia, Humanbody.
[76] Wikipedia, Animal.
[77] Wikipedia, Cellularrespiration.
[78] Wikipedia, Spirit.
[79] Dictionary.com, SpiritDefinitionofSpirit.
[80] Longman Dictionary of Contemporary English, spiritmeaningofspirit.

acquired knowledge and our thoughts and mental capabilities. It is an expression of personality, knowledge, and wisdom. It is what moves our body.

The spirit world of the shamans is not much different from the physical world. Spirits are in everything and everywhere. Spirits have physical bodies; they can fly and travel anywhere with tremendous speed and see and sense things over great distances or in the past or future. Westerners explain such phenomena with the terms telepathy or psychic abilities and talents to sense things using the abilities of the spirits which inhabit human beings. Shamans use spirits during their rituals to fly to other places or sense things far away or in spirit form through the aid of their utha (Heaven power) and other spirit helpers or Ongons.[81]

Because a person's soul is a combination of all that it has experienced before in previous lives, plus our logic, thoughts, emotions and experiences in this life, which are driven by the spirit, that spirt cannot continue after the body's physical death. Its role was to help the soul experience a lifetime of physical existence. At the moment of death, when the soul leaves the corporeal body to be reincarnated, the spirit's work is complete and it does not continue.

8.4. Atman—Hinduism

Atman is a Sanskrit word that means inner self, spirit, or soul. In Hindu philosophy, especially in the Vedanta school of Hinduism, Atman is the first principle: the true self of an individual beyond identification with phenomena, the essence of an individual. In order to attain liberation (moksha), a human being must acquire self-knowledge, which is to realize that one's true self is identical with the transcendent self-Brahman.

The six orthodox schools of Hinduism believe that there is Atman (soul, self) in every being. This is a major point of difference with the Buddhist doctrine of Anatta, which holds that there is no unchanging soul or self.

8.5. Theological Soul

Soul and the spirit are the two primary immaterial parts that Scripture ascribes to humanity.[82] The word spirit refers only to the immaterial facet of humanity. Human beings have a spirit, but we are not spirits. However, the words soul and spirit are often used interchangeably; the primary distinction between soul and spirit is that in men and women the soul has animated life, or is the seat of the senses, desires, affections, and appetites.

The soul, in many religious, philosophical, and mythological traditions, is the ethereal essence of a living being. The soul or psyche comprises the mental abilities of a living being: reason, character, feeling, consciousness, memory, perception, thinking, etc. Depending on the philosophical system, a soul can either be mortal or immortal.[83] The soul is alive, physically and eternally. The spirit can be either alive, as in the case of believers (1 Peter 3:18), or dead as unbelievers are (Colossians 2:13; Ephesians 2:4-5).

Believers in Jesus Christ and his role in salvation respond to the things that come from the Spirit of God, understanding and discerning them spiritually. The spirit allows us to connect, or not, with

---

[81] http://www.face-music.ch/bi_bid/historyoftengerism.html, ShamanismTengerisminMongoliainEnglish.
[82] GotQuestions.org, Whatisthedifferencebetweenthesoulandspiritofman?.
[83] Wikipedia, Soul.

God. Our spirits relate to His Spirit, either accepting his promptings and conviction, thereby proving that we belong to him (Romans 8:16) or resisting him and proving that we do not have a spiritual life (Acts 7:51).

The spirit is the element in humanity that gives us the ability to have an intimate relationship with God. Whenever the word spirit is used, it refers to the immaterial part of humanity that "connects" with God, who himself is spirit (John 4:24).

Judaism and Christianity teach that only human beings have immortal souls, although immortality is disputed within Judaism and the concept of immortality may have been influenced by Plato.

The "origin of the soul" has provided a vexing question in Christianity. The major theories put forward include soul creationism, traducianism, and pre-existence. According to soul creationism, God creates each individual soul created directly, either at the moment of conception or some later time. According to traducianism, the soul comes from the parents by natural generation. According to the pre-existence theory, the soul exists before the moment of conception. There have been differing thoughts regarding whether human embryos have souls from conception, or whether there is a point between conception and birth where the fetus acquires a soul, consciousness, and/or personhood. Stances in this question might play a role in judgments on the morality of abortion.[84]

The most basic meaning of "soul" is "life," there is no distinction as to whether it refers to physical or eternal life. Jesus asks what it profits a man to gain the whole world and lose his soul, referring to his eternal life (Matthew 4:26 p.m.). Both Old and New Testaments reiterate that we are to love God completely, with the whole "soul," which refers to everything that is in us that makes us alive (Deuteronomy 6:4-5; Mark 12:30). Whenever the word "soul" is used, it can refer to the whole person, whether physically alive or in the afterlife.

The soul is our source of absolute uniqueness, a place within that connects you not only to your own value and essence, but to the value and essence of every other living being. This is limiting; we will get back to that later.

8.6. Where Is the Soul in the Physical Body?

Debate on "where" the soul is located in a physical body is a large and disruptive discussion topic. Mostly because we do not have a suitable definition by which to recognize the soul if and when we are lucky enough or astute enough to find it!

- Descartes: The pineal gland is a tiny organ in the centre of the brain that played an important role in Descartes's philosophy. He regarded it as the principal seat of the soul and the place in which all our thoughts are formed.[85]

- Leonardo da Vinci used his experience in the field of anatomy to hypothesize that the soul was located in the optic chiasm, near the third ventricle of the brain. His views were

---

[84] Wikipedia, Soul.
[85] Stanford Encyclopedia of Philosophy, DescartesandthePinealGland.

supported by observations of change in perception following disturbances to that particular area of the brain.[86]

- Aristotle in De Anima (On the Soul) suggests that the organs of the body are required for the soul to interact with. Unlike Plato, Aristotle believed the soul's existence was not separate from the human body; thus, the soul could not be immortal. Similarly, to Plato, however, Aristotle believed the soul is composed of three parts: the vegetative, sensitive, and rational. Growth and reproduction are a result of the vegetative soul, and are found in all organisms. The sensitive soul, however, allows for sensation and movement in humans and animals. Third, the rational is exclusive to humans, and allows for rational thought.[87]

8.7. Ensoulment

After considering "where" the soul can be found in the body, how does it get there, when does it arrive?

In religion, ensoulment is the moment at which a human being gains a soul.[88] [89] Some religions say that a soul is newly created within a developing child and others, especially in religions that believe in reincarnation[90], that the soul is pre-existing and added at a particular stage of development.

In the time of Aristotle, it was widely believed that the human soul entered the forming body at 40 days (male embryos) or 90 days (female embryos), and quickening was an indication of the presence of a soul. Other religious views are that ensoulment happens at the moment of conception; or when the child takes the first breath after being born; at the formation of the nervous system and brain; at the first brain activity (e.g., heartbeat); or when the fetus is able to survive independently of the uterus (viability).[91]

The concept is closely related to debates on the morality of abortion as well as the morality of contraception. Religious beliefs that human life has an innate sacredness to it have motivated many statements by spiritual leaders of various traditions over the years. However, the three matters are not exactly parallel, given that various figures have argued that some kind of life without a soul, in various contexts, still has a moral worth that must be considered. [92]

---

[86] Wikipeda, Historyofthelocationofthesoul.
[87] Wikipeda, Historyofthelocationofthesoul.
[88] Wikipedia, Ensoulment.
[89] https://en.wikipedia.org/wiki/The_City_of_God, TheCityofGod.
[90] http://healerofheartsandminds.com, Reincarnation,PastLives,SufferingandtheBible,AShaman'sViews.
[91] Wikipedia, Ensoulment.
[92] Wikipedia, Ensoulment.

9. Shamanic Soul

The Catholic theologian Thomas Aquinas[93] attributed "soul" to all organisms but argued that only human souls are immortal. Other religions, most notably Hinduism and Jainism, hold that all living things, from the smallest bacterium, to the largest mammals, are the souls themselves and have their physical representative, the body, in the world. The actual self is the soul; the body is simply a mechanism to experience the karma of that life. Thus, if we see a tiger, then there is a self-conscious identity or soul residing in it, and a physical representative of the whole body of the tiger, which is observable in the world. Some teach that even non-biological entities such as rivers and mountains possess souls. This belief is called animism.[94]

Animism is a major part of the shamanic world view and understanding of what this world represents. Shamans often work by being able to reach a different level of consciousness or awareness that allows them to speak to the spirits of the natural world, who can then provide them with knowledge and information. Shamanism often relies pretty heavily on animistic ideas with most shamanistic practices but not all but animism can exist without shamanism.

Your soul resides inside your body in the physical world, but it also lives in the Soul World at the same time. Everyone and everything are in the Soul World because everyone and everything have a soul.

The soul is the principle of life, feeling, thought, and action in humans. In some religions, it is believed that when the person dies, although their body is no longer alive, their spirit or soul moves on to another world. The soul in religion is needed for reincarnation, which is evident in Hinduism and Buddhism, was when we die, our souls come back to take over the body of any living matter. Souls are not only evident in religion but also in philosophy.

9.1. Shamanism and Animism

Shamans have visions and perform various deeds during a trance and it is believed they have the power to control spirits in the body. They may leave normal existence and travel or fly to other worlds. Manchu-Tungus nomads of Siberia and northern Chinese language, Shaman means "agitated or frenzied people."

Shaman are bridges between their communities and the spiritual world. During trances, which are induced during a ritual, shamans seek spirits to help cure illnesses, bring about good weather, predict the future, or communicate with deceased ancestors.
Animism attributes a distinct spiritual essence or soul to plants, inanimate objects, and natural phenomena. It is a belief in a supernatural power that organizes and animates the material universe and that ancestors watch over the living from the spirit world.
There are places on earth where sacred power is concentrated. Those places are held sacred and where communication with the spirit world takes place.

9.2. Bon Sarma

---

[93]
[94] Wikipedia, Soul.

Often referred to as New Bon, this is an eclectic tradition combining elements of Indian Buddhism and Yungdrung Bon, which appeared in the eighth century AD and is still very popular in eastern Tibet, particularly in Kham.[95]

9.3. Mixed Bon

This refers to the wide range of tribal traditions practised in the borderlands surrounding Tibet and the Himalayas, in which Prehistoric Bon, Yungdrung Bon and various other elements mingle in various proportions.[96]

9.4. Bo Murgel

The Bo Murgel belief system of Mongolia and Buryatia—thousands of miles from Tibet—has many features in common with Tibetan Bon, not least of which is its name, Bo—pronounced like "bore" with a double "or" sound. [97]

9.5. Dzogchen

Dzogchen or "Great Perfection," it is a tradition of teachings in Tibetan Buddhism aimed at discovering and continuing in the natural primordial state of being. It is a central teaching of the Yungdrung-Bon tradition as well as in the Nyingma school of Tibetan Buddhism. In these traditions, Dzogchen is the highest and most definitive path of the nine vehicles to liberation.[98] According to this terma, Dzogchen originated with the founder of the Bon tradition, Tonpa Shenrab.

---

[95] Dmitry Ermakov, BOANDBON-ANCIENTSHAMANICTRADITIONSOFSIBERIAANDTIBETINTHEIRRELATIONTOTHETEACHINGSOFACENTRALASIANBUDDHA.
[96] Ermakov, BOANDBON-ANCIENTSHAMANICTRADITIONSOFSIBERIAANDTIBETINTHEIRRELATIONTOTHETEACHINGSOFACENTRALASIANBUDDHA.
[97] Ermakov, BOANDBON-ANCIENTSHAMANICTRADITIONSOFSIBERIAANDTIBETINTHEIRRELATIONTOTHETEACHINGSOFACENTRALASIANBUDDHA.
[98] Wikipedia, Dzogchen.

10. Signs of Soul Loss

To a shaman "soul loss," is a loss of meaning, direction, vitality, mission, purpose, identity, and genuine connection; a deep unhappiness that, unfortunately, most of us have come to consider as simply ordinary. The soul is our source of absolute uniqueness, a place within that connects you not only to your own value and essence, but to the value and essence of every other living being. The soul has not become lost; rather, we have disconnected from it. Trauma, physical, mental, and emotional are the most frequent causes for becoming disconnected from your soul.

Another cause of disconnection is an overwhelming reliance and focus on ego and the thinking mind, which makes no room for any spiritual are emotional time alone with your soul and the energy it has for you. If everything is about achievement for the self, and self is the only focus, when do you stop and smell the roses? When do you stop to watch a bird singing in the tree? When do you give your souls something back for all it has done for you?

What makes soul loss so subtle and dangerous is that very few people have realized that it has happened. Most of us do not know that we have disconnected from our soul and have come to accept as normal a numbness and lack of meaning in our lives. [Lissa Rankin, MD[99]]

Because we all belong to this culture, we all suffer from soul loss. Soul loss is an epidemic and blinds us from seeing the potential for joy and wholeness in ordinary life. When you heal from soul loss, you see familiar things in new ways so you can increase your joy in what you already have. [Lissa Rankin, MD[100]] Diagnostic Signs that indicate soul loss:[101]

---

[99] Lissa Rankin https://lissarankin.com, DiagnosticSignsThatYou'reSufferingFromSoulLoss.
[100] https://lissarankin.com, DiagnosticSignsThatYou'reSufferingFromSoulLoss.
[101] https://lissarankin.com, DiagnosticSignsThatYou'reSufferingFromSoulLoss.

Table 1 - Signs of Soul Loss

#	Description
1	You feel like you're not as good as other people.
2	You yearn to be of service, but you have no idea what you have to contribute and why it matters.
3	You find yourself striving in vain for an impossible-to-achieve standard of perfection.
4	Your fears keep you from living large.
5	You're frequently worried that you're not good enough, smart enough, thin enough, young enough, [fill in the blank] enough.
6	You feel like a victim of circumstances that are beyond your control.
7	You feel like your daily life is meaningless and task-driven.
8	You often feel helpless, hopeless, or pessimistic.
9	You protect your heart with steel walls.
10	You often feel you don't really matter and your love doesn't make a difference.
11	You're always trying to fit in and belong, but you rarely feel like you do.
12	You feel beaten down by the challenges you face in your life.
13	You suffer from a variety of vague, hard to treat physical symptoms, such as fatigue, chronic pain, weight gain or loss, insomnia, skin disorders, or gastrointestinal symptoms.
14	You struggle with being able to accept love and nurturing.
15	You feel depressed, anxious, or chronically worried.
16	You feel like you're not appreciated enough.
17	You find yourself often judging others.
18	You frequently numb yourself with alcohol, drugs, sex, television, or excessive busyness.
19	You feel disappointed with life.
20	You've forgotten how to dream.

11. Soul Retrieval

The human body is the material and physical structure of a human being. It is composed of many different types of Cells that together create tissues and subsequently organ systems. They ensure homeostasis and the viability of the human body. [102]

---

[102] Wikipedia, Humanbody.

It comprises a head, neck, trunk (which includes the thorax and abdomen), arms and hands, legs and feet. [103]

The study of the human body involves anatomy, physiology, histology, and embryology. The body varies anatomically in known ways. Physiology focuses on the systems and organs of the human body and their functions. Many systems and mechanisms interact in order to maintain homeostasis, with safe levels of substances such as sugar and oxygen in the blood. [104]

The body is studied by health professionals, physiologists, anatomists, and by artists to assist them in their work. [105]

It is the physical entity we interact with, on the subway, in the grocery store, at work, in love or when we are in conflict.

The physical body is what we find attractive in a man or woman until we know the person better. It is the physical body that creates limitations, such being confined to a wheelchair, and it grants gifts, such as being artistic or proficient and admired in sports. All of these gifts and limitations are part of the boundary to the learning experience of the soul and in which the spirit must work.

11.1. Other Bodies

Human beings are not the only physical beings that have a body; animals, plants, and cells also have bodies.

Animals are multicellular eukaryotic organisms that from the biological kingdom Animalia. With few exceptions, animals consume organic material, breathe oxygen, are able to move, can reproduce sexually, and grow from a hollow sphere of cells, the blastula, during embryonic development. Over 1.5 million living animal species have been described—of which around 1 million are insects—but it has been estimated there are over 7 million animal species in total. Animals range in length from 8.5 millionths of a meter to 33.6 metres (110 ft). They have complex interactions with each other and their environments, forming intricate food webs. The kingdom Animalia includes humans, but in colloquial use the term animal often refers only to non-human animals. The scientific study of animals is known as zoology. [106]

When we consider the cellular world, cellular respiration[107] is a guide as to the activity in the cell and the world within and without the cell and the life process taking place in it, which is a mirror of what is taking place in human and animal bodies.
The body is a complex organization of cells, bones, and connective tissues, which when taken together inhabit physical space, whether alive or dead, even when cremated, the body ashes take up space. If you reach out with your index finger, you can touch your body and that of other human beings as well as animals and you can use tools such as microscopes to study other life forms.

---

[103] Wikipedia, Humanbody.
[104] Wikipedia, Humanbody.
[105] Wikipedia, Humanbody.
[106] Wikipedia, Animal.
[107] Wikipedia, Cellularrespiration.

Reincarnation[108] is the philosophical or religious concept that the non-physical essence of a living being, the soul, starts a new life in a different physical form or body after biological death. It is also called rebirth or transmigration.[109] Through different lifetimes, the soul gathers different experiences and it expresses Karma, which it carries from one to another, over and over an effort to seek enlightenment and ascendance.

11.2. Spirit

What we call a Spirit[110][111][112] is also incorporeal. If the soul exists within us and gathers experience through lifetime after lifetime, then in each life it is the spirit that gives expression to the soul's acquired knowledge and our thoughts and mental capabilities. It is an expression of personality, knowledge, and wisdom. It is what moves our body.

Because a person's soul is a combination of all that it has experienced before in previous lives, plus our logic, thoughts, emotions and experiences in this life, which are driven by the spirit, that spirt cannot continue after the body's physical death. Its role was to help the soul experience a lifetime of physical existence. At the moment of death, when the soul leaves the corporeal body to be reincarnated, the spirit's work is complete and it does not continue.

---

[108] http://healerofheartsandminds.com, Reincarnation,PastLives,SufferingandtheBible,AShaman'sViews.
[109] Wikipedia, Reincarnation.
[110] Wikipedia, Spirit.
[111] Dictionary.com, SpiritDefinitionofSpirit.
[112] English, spiritmeaningofspirit.

12. Soul Loss and Retrieval of Elemental Energies

In the Tibetan tradition, there is the notion of "soul loss." Although this is an imbalance of the elements, it is greater than the imbalances suffered in normal life. It is a question of degree. Soul loss is a profound loss of elemental qualities. An illness or a mental disorder is more often seen to be the result of the intrusion of a negative force (thought, feeling or entity) resulting in soul loss (a dissociative process). This can be initiated through grief, illness, trauma or the ill-will of another person and a condition of extreme imbalance that usually, though not always, is caused by traumatic external situations and beings.[113]

Shamans are aware the physical symptoms of illness are also to be treated, and herbal medicines are administered by shamans in addition to spiritual healing. The spiritual aspect of the illness, however, is important because the physical symptoms alone are not the true problem. Soul retrieval is usually necessary in cases of severe and chronic illness. The absence of the Ami or suns souls makes it practically impossible for a body to function normally.[114]

Spirits causing illness may be hostile ancestor spirits—Chotgor, or evil shamans—Burkhan.

Chotgor, ancestor spirits, and other less powerful nature spirits can often be cured by singing or waving of the dalbuur (pendant, amulet) over the patient. The disease spirit may also be removed by sucking or pulling gestures—zolgoh that draw it out of the body. More powerful spirits or hostile shamans will require going into a trance.

Burkhan is the most powerful and may need sacrifices to make them go away. The shaman may use knives, a red-hot iron rod, or a bow and arrow to scare the disease spirit away or to blind it with reflected light from his toli—mirror. An Ongon[115] spirit house may be used to catch a spirit in order to keep it from jumping into another person. An Ongon is used to place him in a natural place so the spirit will not return. Some healings actually involve spiritual warfare. A shaman may physically struggle violently with a stubborn spirit, even using weapons, and his spirits fight alongside with him in order to subdue or drive away the intruder. Shamans who routinely aggressively attack other people may lose their status within the community or are even killed.

The ongon is particularly important black shaman: the main function of the khar talynkh or black shaman is to bring people into contact with the ongon, whose spirit they call up "while drumming in a trance." In late-nineteenth century Mongolia, according to Otgony Purev, yellow shamanism revered ongon as well, and every three years yellow shamans gathered in Dayan Deerh monastery in Khövsgöl Province to "renew" these ancestral spirits.
We say that the soul can be stolen by malevolent beings of the eight classes, which are described in section Eight Classes of Being in this book.

These negative, non-physical external beings damage our capacity for positive human qualities. This usually happens during trauma, such as emotional or physical abuse, an accident, loss of a loved one, assault, rape, incest, divorce, surgery, or wartime experiences. The soul part leaves as a protective mechanism. In indigenous cultures, the soul part is retrieved by a shaman shortly after the trauma. In our culture, people can go their entire lifetime without the soul part.[116]

---

[113] Tenzin Wangyal Rinpoche, SoulRetrievalandRelatedIdeas.
[114] http://www.face-music.ch/bi_bid/historyoftengerism.html, ShamanismTengerisminMongoliainEnglish.
[115] Wikipedia, Ongon.
[116] Theinnervoyage.com, SoulRetrieval.

Someone may also lose part of their soul by giving it to a loved one through a desire to share themselves with another. In some cases, part of a soul part may be stolen. [117]

Psychologically, this phenomenon is understood in terms of dissociation, and it is a brilliant survival mechanism for the human psyche. The major characteristic of all dissociative phenomena involves a detachment from reality, rather than a loss of reality as in psychosis.[118]

What has been lost can be retrieved by the shaman through the practice and rituals of Soul Retrieval. The ritual is complicated and requires instruction and teaching by qualified master.

The shaman first needs to speak to and understand the recipient of the soul retrieval. He or she needs to understand what is missing and what has been damaged so that they may undertake the soul retrieval ritual. Some will call this a diagnosis.

During the ritual, the shaman will enter an altered state of consciousness or ASC. This may be achieved by dance, rhythmic drumming, plant-based hallucinogens or alcohol. However, not all shamans use these techniques; each shaman is unique and uses different techniques to reach the state they need to soul journey.

During the soul journey, the Shaman will join with either a main helping spirit or a series of spirits that will aid in the search for the soul, which may be more fragmented. At this point in the ritual, the shaman and helping spirts must determine the state of the soul and/or its fragments and what healing needs to be undertaken before it is given back to the recipient. It also needs to be determined if the souls or fragments are being held hostage by a spirit and what the intention of that spirit is.

The shaman negotiates with the hostage taker in order to get back the soul they are holding on to. A special, separate ritual may have to be completed in order to satisfy the hostage taker. In some situations, a struggle may be undertaken by the shaman and they're helping spirits and the hostage taker to pull back the soul or otherwise free the soul.
In all the activity of searching and possibly struggling with a spirit, the shaman must protect his or her own spirit. Ensure it remains intact and is not damaged by the actions undertaken. The strength of the helping spirits and experience of the shaman in preforming soul retrieval is essential to the success of the ritual.

Once the shaman and their helping spirits have gathered the soul and any fragments and have healed them, they must be returned to the recipient. The traditional reintegration of the soul with the recipient's physical being is through breath. The shaman breathes hard at or on the recipient and matches the intensity with the intention of sending the soul back to them, and focusing on returning their light. The soul or soul fragments at this stage are like lost children being returned to their parents.

Then we support the client to begin the process of integrating this new energy, by first just allowing the energy to sink down into their bones and cells, which go deeply into the recipient.

---

[117] Theinnervoyage.com, SoulRetrieval.
[118] Wikipedia, Dissociationpsychology.

It is the shamanic gift that enables them to reach through to a lost soul, or part of the soul, and guide it back to its primary personality in safety. In shamanic traditions, clients suffering from depression and anxiety may well be seen as suffering from soul loss related to a missing part of oneself, an intrusion of other influences and so forth.

13. Element Retrieval

As with soul retrieval, the elemental energy of a recipient may be lost, stolen or so seriously unbalanced it may appear that a particular element has been taken away.

Sutra, Tantra, and the shamanic vehicles include practices to reconnect us to the positive qualities. This process is not just about having pleasant experiences; it is about connecting to deeper aspects of ourselves. Although ultimately, we need to go beyond the simplicity of positive and negative, until we actually do, positive qualities lead us closer to the experience of the base of existence, while negative qualities distract us and lead further into abstraction.[119]

When elemental qualities are lost, there is a flattening of experience, a loss of richness and resonance. This is similar to the experience of a broken heart. A man or woman loses a spouse or partner in a shocking way, is betrayed or abandoned, and he or she closes the heart. This is a familiar theme in novels and movies: the person can't love because of the fear of being hurt again. The same kind of inner damage can happen when someone loses a child, is raped, witness's brutality, is subjected to brutality, goes through a war, is in a car accident, or loses a house—the catastrophes and calamities that fall upon us humans. The shock to the soul overwhelms it with fear, loss, or some other powerful emotion and, and the result is the loss of positive qualities, the loss of life force and vitality and the loss of joy and empathy. It may also result in physical frailty and the loss of sensory clarity.[120]

Regardless of whether the loss of elemental energy is sudden or occurs over time, or is the result of a traumatizing or dehumanizing environment, the damage to the energy of the elements and their balance in the recipient. The cause is a negative spirit, or spirits.

When we are physically weakened, our physical body is susceptible to bacterial and virus infections from bacteria and viruses. When we are psychically weakened, we are susceptible to the influences of negative non-physical beings.

After an accident, for instance, an individual may experience lethargy, a loss of inspiration and creativity, or a loss of vigour. This condition may heal naturally, but if it doesn't, if fire element energy has been lost, it can become chronic. This may show up in work and in relationships, and may manifest in the body as an illness and in the mind as a disturbance in cognitive activity. The accident is the apparent physical cause of the loss, but the real loss is caused by trauma or can come as the person is weakened and vulnerable to malevolent external beings. In either case, the damage is manifested in the soul.[121]

Element retrieval also refers to the overabundance of an element which causes spiritual imbalance. The shaman must soul journey to discover the source of the abundance and remove it, and, after removing it, the shaman must rebalance the elements and manage any damage done by the time there was the overabundance of the element. If someone is too grounded as a result of the imbalance, the shaman must support the elements of Air and Space, for example.

---

[119] Tenzin Wangyal Rinpoche, TibetanSoulRetrieval.
[120] Rinpoche, SoulRetrievalandRelatedIdeas.
[121] Rinpoche, SoulRetrievalandRelatedIdeas.

14.   Soul Retrieval—an example

I am both a Usui Tibetan Reiki Master and Teacher and a White Shaman.

Recently I was involved in a series of sessions for someone undergoing cancer treatment. The treatment involved radiation treatment and reconstructive surgery. The healing sessions were conducted remotely, partly due to social distancing and lockdown measures enacted to reduce exposure to Covid-19 and because the sessions do not require in-person contact.

The sessions were a hybrid of Remote Reiki and Shaman. Remote connection is with the angels and guides of the recipient as well as their spirit and soul so physical presence is not required.

I find Remote Reiki to be highly beneficial for treatment of the physical presence of recipients. During this part of the session, I am able to visualize the physical existence of the person I am connecting to. The muscles, tendons, and sinews that make the body move and give it strength are apparent and I can concentrate on reducing stress, tightness, and rigidity I find there.

Hands and feet play a big part in how we interact with the physical world. Feet help us move around and hands are what we carry out activities. They can become tired and tired in a way that is far more excruciating and profound than when we come home and kick off our shoes and massage our feet and say, they are tired. The weariness I am referring to is a measure of the emotional and physical tiredness that includes bones and passes through every joint in the feet or hands. Damaged energy can become trapped in the joints, reducing flexibility and producing pain. Releasing this trapped energy and tiredness is not only good for the hands and feet but also the person whose extremities these are and prevents it from causing greater illness later.

In the case of the recipient undergoing radiation and reconstructive surgery, my shamanic connection allowed me to "take away, and flush away," parts of the tumour. Piece by piece the tumour was removed. The recipient was undergoing radiation treatment at the same time and towards the end of the sessions I saw a piece of bone that seemed to have been damaged by the tumour; its inner channels and pathways were exposed, which they should not have been.

The reconstructive surgery took place but a lot of swelling was occurring. In a session it became clear that peace had not been made with the spirits in the part of the body where the surgery took place.

We have a lot of different spirits in our bodies, like the spirits in a Shaman's mirror. Our bodies are a container and home to many spirits other than the main or core spirit and soul. If we hold out our fingers and touch our nose, along with the physical action, the spirits in our hands and nose detect each other and sense the momentary link.

The recipient was unconscious during the surgery; the reaction of the spirits to the cutting of the surgical procedure caused the recipient's soul to shed fragments of itself in "terror" at what was happening and needed to be appeased.

To make peace with the spirits where the surgery had occurred required something as simple as cold water being splashed three times on swollen eyes was requested. Because of sutures and protective antibiotic ointment, splashing water was not possible, but the recipient has able to touch the eyes three times with a finger dipped in cold water. Through my shaman guide, I was able to hear that the spirits found this acceptable. The spirits said they understood and were at peace.

The soul retrieval presented itself to me as an intensely dark void, aka the underworld. Together with my Shaman guide, companion, and protector, a retrieval of the soul fragments in the void started. I could sense the warm and loving soul fragments of the recipient and could sense them being collected by our helping spirits. Together with their help, I was able to bring them back to the recipient's core soul and I expressed my intention of integrating them, which readily happened.

In the next session, it was apparent that some tiny fragments of soul still needed to be retrieved. In my connection with my Shaman teacher and companion, I could see a "sandy beach" in one corner of the void on which the soul fragments rested. They were like brilliant diamonds among the grains of bright yellow sand. As I revealed my intention to pick them up, I could see my fingers reaching out and picking them up, and then putting them in my other hand. When all were all collected, there were only five or six of them. My helping spirits and my Shaman companion accompanied me back to the recipient's soul and again, I expressed my intention of integrating them, which took place.

In life we all have our fears and doubts, pain, anguish and concerns. Our insatiable ego drives us relentlessly to the point where a bright sunny day with blue sky and puffy white clouds can seem depressing and dark because something is missing, or because we allow ourselves to continue to exist in a toxic environment, often in our workplace, where we spent 1/3rd of our waking day.

In every Remote Reiki Session, I connect with the recipient's soul and this allows me to sense how close and how dense is the darkness is around them. Some

This is not soul retrieval but it is material to the recipient's soul. I am able to sense what surrounds the person's soul and spirit and how dense it is. As part of the session, with my Shaman companion, I push back the darkness, set boundaries dark spirits may not cross or try to influence the recipient's soul.

15. Soul Channels

Open your spiritual channels to be a better parent, spouse, partner, friend, teacher, or healer. When you open your spiritual channels, you access wisdom and guidance to become your best self. Your soul has great wisdom, knowledge, and experience of hundreds or thousands of lifetimes and from your spiritual fathers and mothers in Heaven. Your soul has great love and care for you because your physical journey deeply affects your soul's journey. Your own beloved soul is your best friend and one of your best guides.[122]

Open your spiritual channels to receive guidance and wisdom from your spiritual fathers and mothers in Heaven and from the Divine. Soul Language and Translation Soul Language is the universal language. Every soul can communicate with any other soul through Soul Language.[123]

The soul[124] in many religious, philosophical, and mythological traditions is the incorporeal[125] essence, the nonmaterial form of a living being. Soul or psyche (comprises the mental abilities of a living being: reason, character, feeling, consciousness, memory, perception, thinking, etc. Depending on the philosophical system, a soul may be mortal or immortal.

The soul includes other forms of incorporeal essence; it includes our emotions, our will to do something, or not. Our thoughts and our feelings. It is through our soul that we sense hurt and suffering as well as pleasure and enjoyment. Our soul experiences the energy and drive, or discouragement of external stimulus and how we respond to it.

When we collect all these incorporeal reactions to stimulus, we come to life and others around is, human or animal react to us. Some people have good relations with other humans and animals; some do not. This outward expression of the soul becomes what we and others describe as our personality.

To a great extent, the expression of our personality is reinforced by repeated, similar reactions from those around us. External shocks and changes can change our personality. Sudden, unforeseen loss of a loved one, human or animal can be so fundamental that other aspects of our soul come to the surface that had previously not had expression.

Reincarnation[126] is the philosophical or religious concept that the non-physical essence of a living being, the soul, starts a new life in a different physical form or body after biological death. It is also called rebirth or transmigration.[127] Through different lifetimes, the soul gathers different experiences and it expresses Karma, which it carries from one to another, over and over an effort to seek enlightenment and ascendance.

In the Shaman, world view, humans, and animals possess more than one soul; multiple souls are required in order to inhabit a physical body. Throughout Siberia and Mongolia, it is believed that all humans possess at least three souls; some groups such as the Samoyedes believe there are

---

[122] Master Sha Tao Center Honolulu, OpenSpiritualChannelsSoulLanguageandTranslation-HonoluluTaoHealingSoulHealingEnergyHealingMasterSha.
[123] Honolulu, OpenSpiritualChannelsSoulLanguageandTranslation-HonoluluTaoHealingSoulHealingEnergyHealingMasterSha.
[124] Wikipedia, Soul.
[125] Dictionary.com, Incorporeal.
[126] http://healerofheartsandminds.com, Reincarnation,PastLives,SufferingandtheBible,AShaman'sViews.
[127] Wikipedia, Reincarnation.

more: four in women and five in men. Animals also possess two souls: the Ami body soul and the sun's soul, both of which reincarnate.[128]

- The suld soul, which resides in nature after death
- The Ami body soul, which reincarnates
- The sun's soul, which also reincarnates

These three souls reside in the field of energy that envelops the physical body. This sphere has an upright axis within it, pierced by seven holes that correspond to the seven chakras. These are the seven energy points of a human being.

The suld soul resides at the crown of the head, where there is a direct connection to Father Heaven through the small Tenger that is also located there. The other two souls oscillate back and forth through the holes of the body axis in a sine wave pattern. In order to be perfectly balanced, the sons and Ami souls should always be on opposite sides of the axis. When a person becomes excited, the circulation of the souls through the seven holes speeds up, causing the heart to beat faster and thus creating a feeling of high energy or tension. The balance of the suns and Ami's souls can become unbalanced by spiritual attack or physical trauma, such as an accident, but also by beneficial trauma, such as surgery.

In serious cases, the Ami or sons may get knocked out of the body, and if this continues for a long time, this will result in illness or mental confusion. In cases of soul imbalance or loss, a shaman's help is needed to restore order. In this situation, the Shaman will undertake a soul journey and retrieval to retrieve the Ami or sons—see section on Soul Retrieval.

The suld is the most individualized of the three human souls. It lives in a physical body only once, then takes residence in nature. After death it remains around the body for a while, and some groups create Ongon [129] for these souls to live in so that they are kept close by and can aid in protection of the living.

The Ami is the soul that enlivens the body. It is related to the ability to breathe, Amisgal (animals). It returns after death to the World Tree, where it roosts in its branches between Heaven and earth in the form of a bird. Ami souls tend to reincarnate among their relatives. They are under the care of the womb goddess Umai (daughter of Mother Earth), who dispatches them on spirit horses, omisi Morin, to enter the body at the time of birth. While the Ami may be temporarily displaced during illness, the Ami does not leave permanently until after death.[130]

The sun's soul, like the suld soul, contributes to the formation of a person's personality, but carries the collected experiences of past lives within it. The sun is an inhabitant of the lower world between incarnations but may return as a ghost to visit friends or relatives. Erleg Khan[131], ruler of the lower world, is responsible for the disposition of the sun's souls, and determines when and where it reincarnates. If a soul was extremely evil during its life on earth, he may send it to Ela Guren[132], a part of the lower world where souls are extinguished forever. The sun's soul may also temporarily

---

[128] http://www.face-music.ch/bi_bid/historyoftengerism.html, ShamanismTengerisminMongoliainEnglish.
[129] .
[130] http://www.face-music.ch/bi_bid/historyoftengerism.html, ShamanismTengerisminMongoliainEnglish.
[131] Wikipedia, Tengrism.
[132] Wikipedia, Tengrism.

leave the body and sometimes wander as far as the lower world, which may require a shaman to negotiate with Erleg Khan for its return.[133]

The spirits of the ancestors are used in all rituals with Father Heaven and Mother Earth. The shaman tradition sees the soul as consisting of multiple parts, usually three, each of which has a different fate after death. One sub-soul, known as the suld or unen fayenga, remains on earth forever as an ancestral spirit. Ancestral spirits remain in contact with their descendants and other relatives, as protectors and helpers. Their residence will be in a natural place, such as a rock, spring, or tree. They can be called by shamans as helper spirits during rituals; and they usually settle in an ongon (spirit house, shaman tools, or totems).

Ancestors for Mongols are the Blue Wolf or Red Deer and for the Buryat Mongols the mythical Bukh Baabai Noyon (Prince Father Bull). The bear is an ancestor of many Siberian tribes; the Mongolian word for bear is actually baabgai and means "father," too. Genghis Khan is an ancestor spirit for the Mongolian people. He is worshiped as a patron of the nation and a protector of marriage.

---

[133] http://www.face-music.ch/bi_bid/historyoftengerism.html, ShamanismTengerisminMongoliainEnglish.

16. Difference Between Spirit and Soul

The soul and the spirit are energy beings, connected to the physical body during its lifetime. Collectively, they are the "people" we experience at work, on the train, and as the driver of the cab we are travelling in.

As energy beings, connected to a physical body, we must see all three as part of nature and susceptible to the actions of spirits in nature that can directly affect the life energy of an individual, including their immune system, thoughts, and private energy field. When there is an imbalance, either within the person or the person and their natural surroundings, it is necessary to engage an expert healer, a shaman, to re-establish the primordial harmony existing between the person and nature. Rebalancing the harmony of an individual's soul and spirt affects a cure and a healing.

Death brings the soul to the six Bardo states, and the process of rebirth. The spirit is not immortal, unlike the soul. When the soul reincarnates into a new life, it encounters a new spirt that will grow from birth through to adulthood with the physical body. At death, the spirit ceases to exist along with the physical body it has used to help the soul gather experiences.

It is important to remember that when the soul, consciousness, leaves the physical body, it may remain for a while around the body, in a favourite room, or around a favourite person without connecting to the dead body. When the soul leaves its body, it will see it and not necessarily connect with the meaning of it. This sets it apart from the Out of Body Experiences where there is a necessary connection to what is still a physically living body. The connection of soul, spirit, and body disappears in the dissolution stage of dying.

Death is usually a very emotional environment.

People are crying, expressing themselves very emotionally, naming the body, recalling his life and his qualities, his virtues, etc. It may be that competitors or people who did not like him are criticizing, complaining, and glad that he is no longer physically around. But all of this, the good and the bad are gone. Dissolution has reset the counter on the memories and experiences of consciousness.

A Shaman will be called if the emotions of those who knew the soul in physical form are so strong they are holding the soul to the physical realm, causing it to try and reconnect with them. Later, if the soul disconnects but does not complete the process of rebirth, it may wander the physical realm, connecting to people with which it has no purpose, but may, in some cases, cause injury to those living souls and consciousness.

A soul in the Bardo may encounter difficulties with reincarnation, or the karma of the soul may be such that the soul resists reincarnation due to the prospect of suffering it perceives to be waiting for it in a new life. The family of the deceased may engage a shaman to assist a soul in the Bardo with its reincarnation if they are aware of the soul's difficulties, or some other circumstance, such as a death by accident, or suicide causes a soul to attempt to remain on the physical plane. No family member desires the intervention of departed a soul or it reappears in their lives.

A soul that decides to remain in the Bardo and try and influence a new soul not to reincarnate or to accept a bad or poor reincarnation is known as spirits, and may be either a "good or beneficial spirit," or a "malevolent or dark spirit."

Because these souls have not reborn, and are interacting with different souls in the process of their reincarnation or through their actions trying to return to the physical realm they are referred to as "spirits" rather than souls, and often perceived or believed to be dark spirits and take on the role of demons and evil deities.

Other spirits, those of enlightened beings, Buddhas, prophets, or spirits of souls with good karma, may purposefully not reincarnate to help other souls and provide information and protection to the shaman, as the later connects with the upper, lower, and intermediate [physical] worlds on behalf of humans, who cannot do this.

To the shaman, his/her universe includes an upper, middle and lower realm where spirits exist, along with the spirits of ancestors who must be understood and persuaded to help a soul in its current physical incarnation. In these realms, Shaman encounter demons, and dark spirits when they journey into them and into the Bardo to assist souls with their rebirth or to retrieve a soul when it has been lost or part of it has been stolen, and to promote healing for a client. The shaman's protective helping spirits are those souls that have chosen not to be reborn but instead be helping and supportive spirits.

How and why a soul did not cross over and has been in this state for many hundreds of years comes down to the Karma of the soul when it entered the intermediate state between life and rebirth. Souls, Form, and Function

Seven energy points of a human being). The suld soul resides at the crown of the head, where there is a direct connection to Father Heaven through the small Tenger that is also located there. The other two souls oscillate back and forth through the holes of the body axis in a sine wave pattern. In order to be perfectly balanced, the sons and Ami souls should always be on opposite sides of the axis. When a person becomes excited, the circulation of the souls through the seven holes speeds up, causing the heart to beat faster and thus creating a feeling of high energy or tension. The balance of the suns and Ami's souls can be thrown off balance by spiritual attack or physical trauma. In the most serious cases, the Ami or sons may get knocked out of the body, and if this continues for a long time, this will result in illness or mental confusion. In cases of soul imbalance or loss, a shaman's help is needed to restore order.

17. Shaman V's Mediums

The differences between shamans and mediums involve the consequences of the different socioeconomic conditions under which each type of shamanistic healer is found. The shamans were associated with animal Spirits and hunting magic, sickness, and health, reflecting their subsistence patterns as foragers, while mediums were involved in agricultural rituals. Mediums had lower social and economic status than shamans, while shamans had high social esteem derived from their informal political power and preeminent roles in group leadership. Mediums are predominantly women and generally of low social status, as opposed to shamans, who are predominantly men and of high social status. Shamans were also involved in malevolent activities designed to magically harm their enemies; an activity absent among mediums.

The differences between shamans and mediums are particularly seen in the medium's Altered State of Consciousness [ASC], which is characterized by the experience of possession where a spirit is thought to take over the person's behaviour. Although both shamans and mediums undergo experiences during the selection period in which they have illness, involuntary dreams, or visions, full mediums are more likely to continue to have experiences that occur beyond their control or intention.

Although it was believed that sometimes the shamans' Spirits could be out of their direct control, shamans were generally thought to control the Spirits. This is in stark contrast to the mediums, who are generally thought to act under compulsion from the spirit world. Even though the medium generally intends to enter into an ASC, these experiences are thought to involve possession of the medium, who is believed to be controlled by the possessing spirit.

18. Shaman V's a Medicine Man

A medicine man or medicine woman, there is no gender restriction, is a traditional healer and spiritual leader who serves a community of indigenous people of the Americas. Each culture uses their own name, in their respective Indigenous languages, for the spiritual healers and ceremonial leaders in their particular cultures.

In indigenous North American communities, "medicine" usually refers to spiritual healing. This should not be confused with practitioners who employ Native American ethnobotany, a practice that is very common in a large number of Native American and First Nations households.

Ethnobotany is the study of a region's plants and their practical uses through the traditional knowledge of a local culture and people. An ethnobotanist strives to document the local customs involving the practical uses of local flora for many aspects of life, such as plants as medicines, food, and clothing.

A medicine man or woman usually caries a small pouch that contains sacred items. A personal medicine bag may contain objects that symbolize personal well-being and tribal identity. Traditionally, medicine bags are worn under clothing. Their contents are private, and often of a personal and religious nature.

Other terms for Medicine Man/Woman are "medicine people" or "ceremonial people" are sometimes used in Native American and First Nations communities, for example, when Arwen Nuttall (Cherokee) of the National Museum of the American Indian writes, "The knowledge possessed by medicinal people is privileged, and it often remains in particular families."

Native American indigenous people are reluctant to discuss issues about medicine or medicine people with non-Indians. And, in some cultures, the people will not even discuss these matters with members of other tribes. In most tribes, medicinal elders are prohibited from advertising or introducing themselves as such. As Nuttall writes, "An enquiry to a Native person about religious beliefs or ceremonies is often viewed with suspicion."

One example of this is the Apache medicine cord or Izze-kloth whose purpose and use by Apache medicine elders were a mystery to nineteenth-century ethnologists because "the Apache look upon these cords as so sacred that strangers are not allowed to see them, much less handle them or talk about them."

The term "medicine man/woman," like the term "shaman," has been criticized by Native Americans, as well as other specialists in the fields of religion and anthropology.

While non-Native anthropologists sometimes use the term "shaman" for Indigenous healers worldwide, including the Americas, "shaman" is the specific name for a spiritual mediator from the Tungstic peoples of Siberia and is not used in Native American or First Nations communities.

The term "medicine man/woman" has also frequently been used by Europeans to refer to African traditional healers, along with the offensive term "witch doctors." The term "witch doctor is also considered to have a negative connotation, or, its use is intended to belittle or disparage.

A medicine man, or woman's approach to sickness, disease, or misfortune, is to strive to discover the root cause[s] and divine how to prevent the symptoms and conditions from recurring. Rather than the symptoms/cure-based approach of modern medicine. They do this by exploring the supernatural causes of ill health.

There is great emphasis on medicinal plants to heal colds, coughs, fever, asthma, and insect bites. A medicine man/woman is a person with mysterious power over medicine or magic or other mysterious arts in general. The individual is aware that some medicine is good and beneficial in treating an illness, some evil or bad. Bad medicine may be infective, or make the condition worse. It might also be poisonous.

Of all the African religious specialists, medicine-men were the most useful, and people consulted them frequently. They acted as the link between the people and the supernatural realm. Africans believe the cause of ill health, misfortunes, and other afflictions could be traced to the invisible world. Since most of the people did not have the ability to communicate with the forces that controlled that world, the medicine-men became very useful (Magesa 1997,210).

As with other specialists in African Religion, medicine-men/women receive a calling to the profession. Africans believe some were born with the ability, having been born holding divinatory pebbles. The midwives would take note of relevant signs and from the mothers that they had special children. In other cases, a medicine-man would pass on the profession to his son or other younger relative (Mbiti 1969, 167). Yet others received their calls through visions or dreams (Magesa1997,217). In addition, upcoming medicine—men went through training that involved attachment to practising medicine-men. The trainees learned the several ways available of dealing with health issues. Africans believed that medicine men possessed special gifts or powers (Magesa 1997, 219). Through training, they were shown how to utilize those gifts and powers. After training, they were officially installed through a ceremony presided over by a medicine-man.

The cleansing rituals that followed marked a new start in life, symbolized by shaving the hair, lighting a new fire, or sweeping the house ceremoniously. Such rituals may not mean much to an observer… They are psychologically vital and, no doubt, play a great role in healing the sick or helping the sufferer (Ndung'u and Mwaura 2008, 45).

Both Christianity and colonialism in Africa have sought to discredit African psychological healing, which involves promoting the mental and emotional well-being of the individual and the techniques developed for psychological healing have been developed in an African environment to address specific problems. Some Africans afflicted with certain crises can only be addressed using this approach. These afflictions include barrenness, mental disturbances, misfortunes, and the effects of witchcraft and sorcery in humans, combined with unproductive farms and animals (Mumo2009, 63).

Comparing a shaman to a medicine man or woman, there are some notable differences. The shaman soul journeys either for themselves or at the request of another for healing purposes. A soul journey may also be undertaken to retrieve a soul or to help guide a lost spirit or a spirit that has not crossed over into the spirit world. Battles and confrontations with evil or dark spirits and souls may be undertaken to help a sick individual. The shaman's universe includes an upper, middle, and lower realm where spirits exist, along with the spirits of ancestors who must be understood and persuaded to help a soul in its current physical incarnation.

A shaman experiences possession by a spirit guide during a healing ceremony. It is also the case that a spirit guide maybe human or animal, but it is a guide they are familiar with and have a close relationship with.

Generally, a shaman, especially one from Mongolia and Tibet, does very little work with regard to herbs and natural herbal treatments.

19. Shaman V's a Witch Doctor

The word 'witchcraft' elicits the worst stereotypical, virulent, and extremely negative images in most people's minds. There is almost a conditioned reflex to the word. The term automatically evokes and reinforces images of 'ignorance,' 'backwardness,' 'primitive,' 'uncivilized,' 'superstitious,' 'undeveloped.' It tends to confirm deeply ingrained negative opinions of society and the individuals who are known as Witch doctors.

A witch doctor was originally a type of healer who treated ailments believed to be caused by witchcraft. The term which doctor is sometimes used to refer to healers, particularly in regions which use traditional healing rather than contemporary medicine.

In its original meaning, witchdoctors were emphatically not witches themselves, but rather people who had remedies to protect others against witchcraft. Within their tribe or community, a witchdoctor was a user of magic, who, by the use of spells, charms, herbal remedies, and incantations, sought to cure illness, detect witches, and counteract malevolent magical influences. Witchcraft-induced conditions were their area of expertise.

Since the missionaries thought that they were introducing civilization into Africa, they denounced African institutions, including African approaches to healing. They referred to medicine-men and women who were highly respected for their services as 'witchdoctors.' On the attitude of Europeans to African healing, Ndung'u and Mwaura explain that 'the whole process of healing was in the eyes of the missionaries, part of a wide scheme of witchcraft and paganism, and had to be eradicated in order to pave the way for western civilization and the Gospel' (Ndung'u and Mwaura 2008, 46).

'When people see havoc in medical institutions and powerlessness of doctors, they go to healers. There's another point: incurable diseases or oncology. When it's a child, they want to turn the world upside down to cure it. So, people go to healers searching for a miracle. This is not about the level of education of those people who go to healers, but about the level of trust in the medicine offered by the state,'

Whilst no one will deny that the tribes throughout Africa. As a whole, believing in witchcraft does not follow that the witchdoctor himself is feared or that he is the evil person that many people depict him to be. Indeed, among the Shona people, he is a much respected and, I might add, a much beloved person, and—if I may be permitted to make the comparison—he is even regarded with the same attachment that the doctor enjoys in European society.

Most Africans believe will the existence of the witch, and to most people, which denotes a person with an evil spirit capable of causing untold misery, tragedy, and death upon any innocent victim. Again, to the Shona people, which, like the witchdoctor, are spiritually endowed. But with a spirit which operates against the interests of mankind. Which, like the witchdoctor, also inherits a spirit, generally from the mother, and this trait is handed down in the family. The witch-practice witchcraft and is able to manipulate occult forces to the detriment of man—quite the opposite to the witchdoctor, who operates the forces for the good of mankind. Thus, the only difference really between the witchdoctor and the witch is the eternal difference of good and bad.

The fountainhead of the belief in magic and witchcraft is the witchdoctor, and the continuance of this philosophy rests on him. As long as he exists, so long can we accept him" presence as the indication of his people's belief and dependence on magic and witchcraft. Once he goes, this extraordinary ancient philosophy will disappear as well.

The witchdoctor's functions thus extend far beyond the mere prescribing of an herb, albeit this would be an important aspect of his practice. He is the hub around which the magical or spiritual world revolves, giving succour and support to those in need and, at the same time, being the means of ensuring good behaviour.

The role of the witch doctor is very different from the Shaman in this context and is reliant on the existence of a witch, someone who communicates with the spirit world to do harm to others. As with the Medicine Man/Woman, described earlier, many of the attributes of the shaman are not present when discussing witch doctors.

Interestingly, the men and women in Europe are recognized as white witches who practise witchcraft. The only difference from the witch discussed here is that a white which serves the people, and is much sought after to cure their diseases. Therefore, the white witch really corresponds to the African witchdoctor and, in essence, there is no difference between the witchdoctor and the witch except in their handling of the powers of Nature.

20. Black, White and Yellow Shaman

Shamans are the preeminent healers of premodern societies. Their roles as healers include medical and psychiatric functions, addressing physical disease as well as a variety of psychological conditions. Shamanism provides mechanisms for inducing healing through systemic psychological integration using ritual, symbols, and ASC. Shamans' practices represent the evolution of a "holistic imperative," a drive towards more integrated levels of consciousness.[134]

Shamanic traditions produce integrative responses that synchronize divergent aspects of human cognition and identity through several mechanisms, including:

- Using ASC, ritual, and symbols to activate synchronizing brain processes
- the stimulation of processes of lower-brain structures and subconscious aspects of personality and self-incorporating people into community rituals that strengthen social support and identity. These therapeutic processes still have relevance in the modern world, as evidenced by the modern resuscitation of the ancient shamanic practices.[135]

In the beginning ... there were only two types of shaman: "black" and "white." Applying the terms white and black to shamans is often a result of the perspective from which you apply the labels. Many such decisions about labels were and still are made from a Judo-Christian view point rather than the indigenous people who have existed with shaman for millennia.

White shaman refers to those who deliver "good" aims to help or heal, while black shaman refers to those who have negative or "evil" aims to hurt or even kill the victims. As Buddhism arrived in Tibet and the Mongolian steppe, a third type appeared: the "yellow shaman."

---

[134] Encyclopedia.com, Shamans.
[135] Encyclopedia.com, Shamans.

21. Black Shaman

Although white and black shamans sometimes overlapped, black shamans were regarded as the most powerful and also referred to as "warrior shamans" because they battled evil forces, travelled to the underworld and were consulted as military advisors. In wartime, their role was to motivate the soldiers and population in order, hopefully, to secure victory for their own side. It was Black shamans that went on campaign with the Mongol armies, or with the tribal forces when battling other tribes. Black Shaman obtained their power from the North, possibly the North Pole or the North Star, and could be easily identified as they always wore black robes with very little, if any, decoration. The primary function of the black shaman was to deal with demons and the dark gods on behalf of their clients. In this role, they were hired to curse their enemies and blight their crops and livestock.[136]

In peacetime they acted as diplomats, political advisors and emissaries and they oversaw the preparation and signing of treaties with the appropriate magical rites. Black shamans were greatly feared, even after their deaths. In the 19th century, when a famous one died, she was placed in a coffin made from the "unclean" wood of an aspen. Her corpse was then nailed down with aspen stakes so she could not become a "night walker" and haunt the living.[137]

Black Shamans maybe malevolent sorcerers who masquerade as real shamans and who entice tourists to drink ayahuasca in their presence. Shamans believe one of the purposes for this is to steal the drinker's energy or power, of which they believe every person has a limited stockpile.[138]

During their initiation, a Buryat[139] Black Shaman must take ninety-nine oaths, which prevents them from causing any kind of harm. She said; it was prohibited to endanger human life and put obstacles in people's way and quarrel, but they had to help all the living creatures.[140] Black shaman from other ethnic groups and tribes are not obliged to take such oaths.

The costume worn by a Black shaman is considered their armour against attacks by black or harmful spirits. The costume includes miniature iron weapons believed to have been forged by Damdin Dorlig, the patron deity of blacksmiths, who is also regarded as an armourer of shamans.

The longer a Black Shaman has practised the more and varied will be iron weapons they will have on their costume. This is because the more experienced Shaman will encounter stronger and more varied dark spirits in their work to expel dark spirits from a client.

---

[136] https://www.newdawnmagazine.com/articles/secrets-of-siberian-shamanism, SecretsofSiberianShamanism.
[137] https://www.newdawnmagazine.com/articles/secrets-of-siberian-shamanism, SecretsofSiberianShamanism.
[138] http://situgen.blogspot.com/search/label/shaman%27s%20costume, shaman'scostume.
[139] https://en.wikipedia.org/wiki/Buryatia, Buryatia.
[140] http://situgen.blogspot.com/search/label/shaman%27s%20costume, shaman'scostume.

22. White Shaman

White shamans obtain their magical power from a westerly direction, the home of the benevolent deities and spirits. They operated at a tribal level almost exclusively as healers and diviners and they only had dealings with beneficent entities. It was their role to pacify angry or evil spirits, exorcise them if they possessed human beings and help the tribe live in harmony with their natural environment and the spirit world. To this end, on a physical level, they were often employed in an administrative role to oversee tribal affairs.[141]

By contrast to the Black Shamans, who epitomized courage and iron discipline, the White Shamans personified humanity. Instead of pitting force against force and bad against bad, like the Black Shamans, the White Shamans had a set of beliefs and customs related to White deeds, habits, and thoughts. In ancient times, the White Shamans created rituals that called upon the peaceful masters or spirits of the White Side; only directing their worship and prayers in this direction. Consequently, Mongolian shamans became divided into black and white factions.[142]

According to the surviving sources, White Shamans were relatively numerous. In general, they carried out activities and rituals concerning the general direction peoples' lives were taking: most directly through keeping public and administrative order. They instructed people to commune with nature, water, and earth spirits; pacifying angry spirits and undoing the damage they caused. White Shamans also cared for the health of the people.[143]

White Shamans do not use the same tools as Black shaman; for example, they do not sue a drum. Instead they walk with a wooden staff and ring bells during ceremonies. There are also differences in the costume worn by White Shamans. They do not wear antlered headdress; instead they wear a cape called a nemerge.

Buddhist Lamaism was the main cause of the decline in the numbers of White shamans. During the 17th to 19th centuries, the White shaman tradition suffered most among the Khalkha and Barga tribes, and throughout Inner Mongolia. In present day, white shamanism is returning.

---

[141] https://www.newdawnmagazine.com/articles/secrets-of-siberian-shamanism, SecretsofSiberianShamanism.
[142] https://mongolianstore.com/the-black-shamans/, TheBlackandWhiteShamans.
[143] https://mongolianstore.com/the-black-shamans/, TheBlackandWhiteShamans.

23. Yellow Shaman

Yellow shamanism is the term used to designate a particular version of shamanism practised in Mongolia and Siberia, which incorporates rituals and traditions from Buddhism. "Yellow," indicates Buddhism in Mongolia, since most Buddhists there belong to what is called the "Yellow sect" of Tibetan Buddhism, whose members wear yellow hats during services. The term also serves to distinguish it from a form of shamanism not influenced by Buddhism (according to its adherents), called "Black Shamanism."[144]

The term "yellow shamanism" was first introduced in 1992 by Sendenjav Dulam and its use was then adopted by Otgony Pürev, who considers it to b4e the Buddhism-influenced successor of an unbroken practice that goes back to Genghis Khan—that earlier practice was "black shamanism" and was practised by the Darkhad in defiance of the Buddhism introduced to the area by the Khalkha. According to Pürev, the centre of yellow shamanism was the Dayan Deerh monastery in Khövsgöl Province, where he found evidence of yellow practices in the recitations and prayers of a shaman born in the province in 1926; he argues that yellow shamanism has by now ceased to exist anywhere.

Between the 17th and 19th centuries, Lamaism and Tibetan Buddhism[145] imposed itself on the people of Mongolia. Although not the state religion as it was in Tibet, Buddhist persecution made it very difficult for shamans of all beliefs. Black shamans who refused to submit to the foreign religion. White shamans were divided. Some submitted to Buddhist authority and became Yellow shamans. Other White shamans refused to give up their traditions. These shamans were thrown into the "Black" category by the Lamaists.[146] Therefore, both Black and White shamans were in the same category between the 17th and 19th centuries.

Yellow Shaman were those who are controlled by Buddhist Lamas, and practised shamanic rituals and traditions in conjunction with Tibetan Buddhism.

After the establishment of the Great Mongol Empire of Chinggis Khan, his Borjigin clan became the Golden (Imperial) clan, towering above all Mongol clans. The Lord-Spirits, the Protector-Spirits, the Guardian-Spirits of the BorJigin clan were raised to the high rank of the Ancestor-Spirits of the whole nation of Mongols.

The establishment of Buddhism in Mongolia and the adoption of Buddhism by the Borjigin clan resulted in White Shamans and Shamanesses willingly accepting the new Yellow Religion, "Yellow" being the Saffron colour of Buddhist robes. White Shamans and Shamanesses embracing Buddhism received the title "Yellow Shamans and Shamanesses." Black Shamans and Shamanesses did not/do not accept Buddhism.
Many of these Yellow Shamans and Shamanesses had the books of shamanist prayers and hymns in Mongolian transcribed by monks with the Tibetan syllabic characters in the form of Buddhist books of prayers, and the monks and Yellow Shamans believed that a Mongol text transcribed with Tibetan characters is eight times more blessed than the same text written in Mongol letters.[147]

---

[144] Wikipedia, Yellowshamanism.
[145] Wikipedia, TibetanBuddhism.
[146] Wikipedia, TibetanBuddhism.
[147] Yönsiyebü Rinchen, "White, Black and Yellow Shamans Among the Mongols," *Ultimate Reality and Meaning* 4, no. 2 (1981), https://doi.org/10.3138/uram.4.2.94.

Because of this, the distinction between the two traditions was Muddied in Lamaist dominated regions. Luckily, the tribes in the Northwest regions, such as the Darhad and Urinahai, had close contact and solidarity with Siberian peoples, such as the Tuvans and Buryats, who kept their traditions intact.

Communism in Mongolia stopped the Buddhist atrocities, but was a step backwards for freedom of religion. When Mongolia changed to a democracy in the 1990s, shamanism grew stronger in the region again.

Table 3 The Buddhist concept of 9 levels of Consciousness.

Conciousness	Physically	Description	
1st Level	Sight	What we See	
2nd Level	Hearing	What we Hear	
3rd Level	Smell	What we Smell	
4th Level	Taste	What we Taste	
5th Level	Touch	What we Touch	
6th Level	The 6th Sense integrates the first five levels of Consciousness into a whole. We make judgements and take action here. This is our consciousness mind		
7th Level	The intuitive realm where we self identify and distinguish ourselves from others		
8th Level	Our Karmic energy store house. It is here the latent causes and effects of our thoughts, words and deeds accumulate. This level is eternal.		
9th Level	Pure life force, the power to live . . . It is the greater self that works for the happiness of all		

"White shamans," have returned and are no longer forced into the "Yellow" category. The "Yellow" category is no longer a shaman classification.

24. Levels of Consciousness

Note: The eighth level of consciousness transcends the boundaries of the individual and interacts with the karmic energy of others, merging with the latent karmic energy of one's family, ethnic group and humankind, and even with that of animals and plants.

This explains how one person's inner transformation, or human revolution, can change the destiny of a family, society, and humanity.

25. Sacred Directions

In an age when there were no compasses, Shamans looked to the direction in which the sun rose and set and the North Star to know which way they're facing. They would look from North to

Table 4 The Five Elements and Sacred Directions

Color	Symbolizes	Negative emotions	Properties	Sacred Direction[s]	Mongol Interpretation	Meaning
Blue	Sky and Space	Ignorance	Accommodates all other elements	Up		Sky and Cosmos
White	Air and Wind	Anger	Motion	East	Female, disease and discord	Cardinal Direction: Air and the Power of Mind
Red	Fire	Desire	Temperature	South	Front	Cardinal Direction: Fire and the Power of Action
Green	Water	Jealousy	Cohesion	West	Male, Benevolent spirits	Cardinal Direction: Water and the Power of Emotions
Yellow	Earth	Pride	Solidity	North	Behind	Cardinal Direction: Earth and the Power of Body
				Down		Planet and Sacred Place
				Center [within yourself]		Direction of Spirit
				Axis North / South		Balance between reflective sensing and the active doing
				Axis East / West		Balance between thinking and feeling, or analysis and intuition
				Axis Up / Down		Attunement to the home Planet and attunement to the beyond

south, where the south would be.Come the "front" and North was "behind." The right side, i.e., west, was the male world and home to benevolent spirits. East, the direction the sun rose was female and home to spirits that bring sickness and discord.

25.1. Five Elements

The five elements in Tibetan Shamanism are space, air, fire, water, and earth. In Tibetan philosophy, these elements are symbols of the fundamental forces that compose all phenomenal appearances. These elements create an organized system and are central to most accounts within Tibetan Buddhism.

Tibetan prayer flags are bright and beautiful, but their colours aren't just for show. Each hue signifies an element—and the flags are always arranged in a specific order, from left to right: blue, white, red, green, and yellow. Blue represents the sky, white represents the air, red symbolizes fire, green symbolizes water, and yellow symbolizes earth. All five colours together signify balance.

Table 2 Tibetan Shamanism: Elements & colours

Elements	Colour
Space	Blue
Air	White
Fire	Red
Water	Green
Earth	Yellow

A person is a blend of these elements, and to be truly healthy, their energies in these elements need to be balanced in the person.

These five elements—space, air, fire, water, and earth—are symbolic of the fundamental forces that are integral to all phenomena. As the body is developing in the womb, earth provides support, water provides cohesion, fire causes maturing, wind, air causes development, and consciousness. The element of space provides spaciousness to form the body.
In Tibetan Buddhism and in Tibetan culture, life is seen through these five elements, which continually increase and decrease in relation to one another. This view forms the basis of medicine, astrology, the calendar, and psychology, and it underlies Tibetan traditions of shamanism, Tantra, and Dzogchen.

25.2. Earth

The earth element is the densest expression in form, the most materially present, and is related to qualities of stability, hardness, and heaviness.

Find a place where you can be quiet and sit. For myself. This is a favourite bench close to a large lake. The lake speaks to the element of water, which comes later. In the warm weather, I will be wearing sandals and I will take them off and allow my feet to rest on the ground.
Clear your mind of all worries and try to shut out or simply ignore people and even animals around you. Connect and draw energy from the earth under your feet. I found that, even in the cooler fall weather, the ground was "warm" to my bare feet. I also found that pains I had felt in my feet and lower legs went away and stayed away.

This connection to the earth is also known as a grounding exercise. You are grounding yourself and your psyche to something solid, the earth element.

If you are unable to find a suitable place to connect with earth, if you have plant pots in which plants are growing, rest your finger tips or your hands on the earth and concentrate on how it feels.

Earth element is stable. Always stable. If you are annoyed or angry at something or someone, focus on the stability of the earth element to reduce and eliminate your anger.

25.3.   Water

In my earth exercise, I sat next to a large body of water; without knowing it, I was completing the water service at the same time as my earth exercise.

While I was fortunate to be close to a large lake, the water in your bath, your shower, or what you drink, drink the water slowly. All will help you feel and understand the water element.

Water, even a glass of water, has enormous power and potential. It is cool and it is warm. It is deep and peaceful until agitated by wind or a spoon stirring in your glass.

Water is the beginning of cohesive form; it is fluid and takes on the shape of any vessel it is in. Place drops of water close to each other on a flat surface, a little movement and the drops will come together and effortlessly combine.

There is no struggle; one drop does not negotiate with another as to whether they should combine or not and no loss of identity. Two drops simply become one.
Your body is mostly water, connected with the element of water, especially that in your own body. If you are in your bath or under your shower, feel how comforting and relaxing it is. If you swim, it will hold you up.

If you are angry or frustrated, Slow down and relax. Let the element of water remove your tensions and take them away. It is comforting, and like earth, it brings stability to you. Be like the water in the container, quiet and passive, allowing the situation to flow over you.

25.4.   Fire

The place where I sit with my shows off drinking in the consistency and strength of earth and water also happens to be a very sunny place. I can sit there, close my eyes, feel the earth, and listen to the water while the warmth of the sun beams down on me.

In winter, sit before a fire place with a fire burning, if you can. If you cannot burn fuel, a stove, a heater, and even your oven while you are cooking is giving off fiery heat—careful not to burn yourself!

Concentrate on the feeling of heat on your face, arms, legs, etc., bring the feeling of heat into your body through the blood; it flows around the muscles, sinews, ligaments and organs.

In your psyche, fire helps you grow by ripening and maturing your thoughts and feelings. It burns negatives and negativity. Fire speaks to creativity and energetic achievement. Typing on a computer speaks to fire! It brings reality and new interesting things into being.

Fire is also related to digestion and nourishment, the result of which creates the fuel to help your muscles move and stay strong.

If you feel dull, uninspired, listless, or unmotivated. Think of the energy of the fire elements and bring it into your body, into your limbs and your intention.

25.5. Air

Air is flowing, movement strength and force. A strong wind that really has no substance can blow over a strong tall tree as well as a building if it is not built well or insecure.

Again, by the lake, where I experience earth, water, and fire, I can also feel wind on my face. It is moving unseen and unheard from the water to the land and yet I feel and sense it.

Think of anger, discomfort, fear, unhappiness and even minor illness such as a headache. Negative thoughts and fears. Those thoughts and fears will make you unhappy, fall down or depressed. Let the wind blow those away and leave your psyche clean and clear and refreshed.

Air drives sailboats and planes fly on it, and in it. So, do birds and the scent of flowers and seeds seeking a new home in the earth in which to grow.

Air is freedom, flexibility, and ease. Let it lift your spirits with the energy and freedom it offers. Think of air and its ease and internalize it. When you are in a situation that is constricting, limiting, think of air and let it blow those things away and lift your mood and your intention.

25.6. Space

Space is above our heads; we can look up on a clear night and see the stars, the moon, and the space between the stars. Let yourself be open to the wonder you are seeing and relax. Let the infinity of the space you are looking at come into your being and give you a sense of limitlessness.

Space forces open any tight, constricted places inside you and dissolve away worries. The more and more you integrate with space, the more you are open to opportunities and the bigger your horizons become, you feel less limited or confined.

When you concentrate on space, your mind is clearer, less cluttered and more energetic. You have less tension, you feel less disrupted. You can sit back and see the big picture and, at the same time, seize the opportunities coming to you because you have more space to accommodate them.

25.7. Imbalance of Elements

Imbalance can manifest itself in the physical dimension. A person with too much earth might be fat or overweight. They may feel devoid of energy and be lazy, dull, or depressed.

They maybe forgetful, slow, or have very little progression in their personal or spiritual development.

The imbalance of the elements from the Dzogchen perspective is subtler. A person may lack stability in meditation, lack awareness of their connection to the base, lack of concentration and lack of understanding of sunyata.

Maybe a person is very unbalanced in a sense of the elements in Dzogchen, but he or she might not notice it because there's nothing particularly wrong physically or psychologically.

If you often feel confused or encounter problems, it may be a lack of stabilizing earth. A lack of creativity means you are lacking fire. A lack of openness, if you feel, as if life is stopping you from speaking up is a lack of space. Someone who is inflexible lacks air.

Too much of any one element can cause problems Look at the kinds of qualities you are giving to others and your own situation. At those times, look within yourself to get a deeper understanding of the emotional level.

25.8. Five Elements and Sacred Directions

The five colours of the five elements appear everywhere. Traditionally, prayer flags come in sets of five: one in each of five colours. The colours are arranged from left to right in a specific order: blue, white, red, green, and yellow. The five colours represent the five elements and the Five Pure Lights.

25.9. At Birth

At birth, we have a good sense of balance in the five elements. Life as they say, takes its toll. We have so many experiences, some bad, some good. There are so many and some are intense, others not so much. But with so many, we do not always process the experiences and we may become overwhelmed or a tragic event just can't be stopped from leaving poorly grounded.

If you have a profound experience and your sense of balance is equally strong, you will be able to deal with it and remain in balance. Being able to process means that you can feel it anyway, but it will not damage you. It will not change you. It will not weaken you. It will not make you lose some qualities. Being able to process means that it will energize you. You are clear with it. In some sense, it can make you grow, make you expand your consciousness and make you become wiser and more understanding.

Not being able to process a shocking event will shake you. If you are a strong person and you are hit by that experience, Maybe you were happy; when you face it, it will take your happiness away. Somehow it will damage that quality.

The five negative emotions of anger, desire, ignorance, jealousy, and pride are related with the elements, too. Anger is related with air. Desire is related to fire, and so on. When one is more balanced, one can have more experience of love.

When one is unbalanced because of too much air and a lack of earth or grounding, one can have an experience of anger instead. Anger feels like an explosion outward, like air blowing things away—you lose control. This is opposite the experience of when you get depressed, because of too much earth and not enough air.

25.10. Sentient Being in Each Element

To the shaman, each of the five elements contains independent, living, sentient spirits. They are non-physical beings with whom he can make contact. The spirits may support us, deny us, or be neutral. Purchasing land, buying plants, and caring for a pet all bring us into contact with the spirits of that element or that animal or plant.

When a bird makes a nest in a tree, they are building there. That is where they will bring up their family just as we look to the land with the intent of building our home to raise our family. The bird will fight other birds for the nesting space and their nest. There are insects, fish, and burrowing animals that also look to the land for their home. They will also fight for the right to retain their space and their art of that land.

Cutting down the tree smashes the birds' home, destroys its eggs and kills its young. Bulldozing the ground destroys the burrows of animals that nest underground. Yet these are physical beings we can see and hear, the non-physical beings we do not. Yet they have the ability to hinder the building process or make it go smoothly. A hindrance from the Earth Element might be unexpected problems with the ground, rocks, or underground streams, which indicate the water element is unhappy as well. Disagreements, accidents, or illness in the construction team. If great progress in construction is made and the team is energized and working well together, we can say everything is going smoothly.

To assist with the construction of the house, for example, connecting with, explaining and asking for permission before changing the ground, the trees, and the water and animals in, under and on the land, we have just purchased. And don't forget, a new house consumes space and changes the way the wind blows across the land where we have built. The deities and spirits for these elements will also need to be considered and engaged with.

After we have made the changes we planned, a ritual of thanks can be held quietly by ourselves is very appropriate. Never forget to say thank you to the spirits and deities we have had dealings with.

Developing this sensitivity and appreciation of the elements, deities, and spirits is part of each of our journeys to recognize the planet is both alive and it is sacred.

25.11. Eight Classes of Being

In Tibet, beings on each class listed below are known to have characteristic appearance, temperaments, and how they relate to humans.

From:
The Rigpa Shedra[148] and the Chinese Buddhist Encyclopedia[149]

---

[148] Rigpa Wiki, Eightclassesofgodsanddemons.
[149] Chinese Buddhist Encyclopedia, Eightclassesofgodsanddemons.

Table 5 Eight Classes for Being

Name	Tibetan Name	Description
Du	Bdud	The four maras (sometimes also translated as "demons") which create obstacles to practitioners on the spiritual path. It is important to understand that they have no inherent existence and are only created by the mind.
Rakshasa	Srin Po	is a kind of malignant spirit that eats human flesh.
Mamo	Ma Mo	Wrathful feminine deities forming part of Ekadzati's entourage. The mamos are considered to be among the main natural forces, which may respond to human misconduct and environmental misuse by creating obstacles and disease.
Naga	Klu	Serpent Spirits live beneath the surface of the earth or in the water, and in trees or rocks, and are believed to be endowed with magical powers and wealth, as well as being responsible for certain types of illnesses (Wyl. klu'i nad) transmitted to humans.
Ging	Ging	are minor deities who attend to the main deities in some wrathful mandalas. They appear as skeletons who beat a drum, wear a triangular pennant pinned in the middle of their hair, and ear ornaments that look like colourful fans.
Rahula	Sgra gcan 'dzin	The Buddha's son, who also became the tenth of the Sixteen Arhats.
Tsen	btasan	Red spirits that haunt rocks are all male, the spirits of erring monks of earlier times. When they are subdued by a great practitioner, the Tsen often becomes the guardian of temples, shrines, and monasteries. Red offerings are made to them.
YakSha	gnod Sbyin	The name of a broad class of nature spirits, usually benevolent, who are caretakers of the natural treasures hidden in the Earth and tree roots.

25.12. Four Levels of Guests

In a Shaman's ritual, he/she considers the level of the guests invited to attend a ritual or ceremony; there are guidelines on how to relate to each.

Table 6 Four Levels of Guests

Guest	Description
First Level	- Fully enlightened beings—very powerful - Buddha's and Bodhisattvas - Free of Ignorance - They have perfected the five wisdoms - We do not control these guests - We ask for their blessings
Second Level	- Not fully enlightened but powerful - From the god realm, they make up the retinue of the major deities' guardians and dharma protectors - They may be from the realm of existence. Such as Angels. - Beings representing the planets and celestial bodies - Second level guests help with healing. - We treat them with respect and honour them
Third Level	- Beings we have karmic connections with - Karmic connections can mean friends and also enemies—in this lifetime and in past existence. - A connection may also mean something that has to be completed. It could be a duty or obligation to another spirit, by the spirit that is in us. This obligation is often referred to as a Karmic Debt.
Fourth Level	- Guests of compassion - They are weaker than we are; they can benefit from our help. - In the BON shamanic tradition, it is important to develop compassion as foundation for our practice.

25.10. Making offering to the Guests

In all the religious traditions of Tibet, offerings are made to spiritual, non-physical beings.
The Mandala offering is foundational to Bon and four schools of Tibetan Buddhism and is made to the first and second level quests.

Other offerings for specific rituals may be Torma, Alcohol, texts, and prayers; these can be especially long prayers or mantras, jewels and precious stones. Also, acceptable is left over food, or food is not prepared or nothing is left over; use of the mind to prepare and gift an imaginary offering is also acceptable.

While we prepare offerings for an important ritual, such as soul retrieval, or healing, we should also not forget to make offerings when everything is going well. Maintaining health, harmony, love, and happiness are important things in our lives. Preparing offerings to sustain spirits and our happy state is important. We do not want blockages to appear; we want to ensure we prevent obstacles from manifesting that may block us tomorrow. If nothing more, we are honouring our protectors and guides.

25.11. Chang-Bu Offering

It is a simple offering made of flour and water. It is called Chang-Bu or a fingerprint Torma.

A shaman may make and use it, but this can also be made by yourself.

Mae, the dough so that is not too wet, it must not be sticky. Think of toothpaste; that consistency is a good guide for the consistency of the Torma. If you are male, lightly oil the right hand; if female, oil the left hand.

Roll the dough until it is a fat roll.

Press the dough into the palm of the oiled hand sufficiently hard that the tough will take on all the ridges, seams, and channels of the skin. Make sure the palm is covered as well as the fingers and thumb. The five fingers and thumb represent the five elements; we want to capture the creases of the fingers where they flex and bend.

Touch the dough to any part of the body that needs healing. This draws spiritual attention to that spot; prana follows the attention, since mind and prana always move together. With the attention on a single part of the body, sensation in that part increases.

We can experience this by touching any place on our bodies and putting our attention there. When this is done with the Chang bu, we use our imagination to draw the illness, trauma, or negativity into the dough.

Try to feel a release in that area of the body. Move the Torma to another part of the body that needs healing. When we have finished, we have a substantial symbol of our illnesses, one that is energetically connected to us; this is offered to the third and fourth guests, the beings who may be causing and maintaining the illness.

The intent behind the ritual is not only to remove the influence of the spirit from the body, but also give the spirit something, which is done through the offering. What is given has some of the energetic properties of the illness but it is now in a purer form that will nourish and satisfy the spirit? When it accepts the offering, it leaves the person whom it has afflicted.

After the ritual is finished, the offering is taken outside and thrown in the direction opposite the individual's birth year sign, the direction, it is believed, in which the negative force is most likely to originate. (If you don't know your sign, refer to the chart at the end of this book.)

Traditionally, after a ritual like this, we look for a dream that signifies success, such as a dream of insects, animals, liquid, or other beings or negative substances coming out of the body.

25.12. The Twelve Astrological Signs and their Directions

Your Tibetan Astrological sign is based on the year of your birth and follows a twelve-year cycle based on the Lunar Calendar. [150]

The duration of one lunar day is from one moonrise to another, and the entire lunar days in the lunar cycle - 29 or 30, depending on the speed of the moon. Since the lunar day does not coincide with sunny days, the lunar day can begin at any time—in the morning, in the afternoon, in the evening or at night. It is important to consider the fact that the lunar day, as a rule, has different durations and sometimes can last only a few hours. The lunar cycle passes through the four main lunar phases: the new moon, the first quarter, the full moon, and the last quarter.
These phases of the moon since ancient times, have been noted in all lunar calendars. The first lunar day is counted from the moment of the new moon.

To determine the opposite direction to the year of your sign, select your sign as 1 [number one], then count to 7 [number 7] that gives you the opposite of your birth sign.

Table 7 Lunar Calendar

Lunar Calendar	Gregorian Calendar	Tibetan Birth Sign	Direction
1914, 1926, 1938, 1950, 1962, 1974, 1986, 1998, 2010, 2022 and 2034	Feb. 1, 2022 – Jan. 21, 2023	Tiger	East – closer to Northeast
1915, 1927, 1939, 1951, 1963, 1975, 1987, 1999, 2011 and 2023…	Jan. 22, 2023 – Feb. 09, 2024	Hare	East – closer to Southeast
1916, 1928, 1940, 1952, 1964, 1976, 1988, 2000, 2012 and 2024…	Feb. 10, 2024 – Jan. 29, 2025	Dragon	Southeast
1917, 1929, 1941, 1953, 1965, 1977, 1989, 2001, 2013, 2025, 2037…	Jan. 29, 2025 – Feb. 16, 2026	Snake	South – closer to Southeast

---

[150] moonhoroscope.com/lunar-birthday, Lunarbirthday.

Table 7 Lunar Calendar

Lunar Calendar	Gregorian Calendar	Tibetan Birth Sign	Direction
1918, 1930, 1942, 1954, 1966, 1978, 1990, 2002, 2014 and 2026...	Feb. 17, 2026—Feb. 05, 2027	Horse	South—closer to Southwest
1919, 1931, 1943, 1955, 1967, 1979, 1991, 2003, 2015, 2027, 2039 and 2051...	Feb. 6, 2027—Feb. 25, 2028	Sheep	Southwest
1920, 1932, 1944, 1956, 1968, 1980, 1992, 2004, 2016 and 2028...	Jan. 26, 2028—Feb. 12, 2029	Monkey	West—closer to Southwest
1921, 1933, 1945, 1957, 1969, 1981, 1993, 2005, 2017 and 2029...	Feb. 13, 2029—Feb. 02, 2030	Garuda—Chinese = Rooster	West—closer to Northwest
1922, 1934, 1946, 1958, 1970, 1982, 1994, 2006, 2018, 2030 and 2042...	Feb. 3, 2030—Jan. 22, 2031	Dog	Northwest
1923, 1935, 1947, 1959, 1971, 1983, 1995, 2007, 2019, 2031, 2043...	Jan 23,2031 Feb 0,2032	Pig/boar	North—closer to Northwest
1913, 1925, 1937, 1949, 1961, 1973, 1985, 1997, 2009, 2021, 2033...	Feb. 12, 2021—Jan. 31, 2022	Elephant—Chinese = Ox	Northeast
1948, 1960, 1972, 1984, 1996, 2008, and 2020	January 25, 2020, to February 11, 2021	Rat	North—Closer to Northeast

26. Altered States of Consciousness [ASC]

Altered States of Consciousness generally include changes in both the content and functioning of the consciousness, usually experienced by an individual and observed by others watching him. The term "state" is not to be trivialized but denotes the states or stages of behaviour through which the individual progresses. Frequently persons in these states appear to be in a sleep like condition commonly referred to as a trance.[151]

A shaman learns and trains how to control their state of consciousness at will. This is necessary because they deal with spirits, of all types; they are a form of energy and the shaman must engage with them in their domain, as a form of energy in their own right.

Shamanic consciousness permits a shaman to view their surroundings as a Non-Ordinary Reality—NOR. While the shaman is aware of what we call everyday reality, i.e., the world of humankind, he/she is also engaged with the abstract world of Nature and natural energies as well as what we call spirit. This level of intense consciousness brings awareness to all worlds, or realities of the upper, middle, and lower world simultaneously.

The Lower World is a world of energy, raw and full of dynamic potential. It is beneath us in the Judeo-Christian belief system; it would be Hell, but in shamanic terms, it is not. It is a world of animal, plant, and echoes of matter's origin. Journeys to the Lower World are often associated with animal guides, power animals, discussions with trees, forests, mountain ranges, continents, etc., lower world is where we meet our most profound mentors and have the most transformative insights. While the Lower World is beautiful and strange, it is also scary. Unfamiliar and powerful creatures exist there and when visiting the realm, we must be on our guard not to be trapped or contaminated.

The Middle World is the energetic and observational analogue of our physical world. In this world or reality, we exist closest to ourselves but a copy of ourselves which struggles and manages the same issues as we do. Remote viewing, seeing, visiting and projections are all conducted mainly in the Middle World.

The Upper World is the realm of Spirit; Spirit is used here not spirits in multiple, although this is where they dwell too. It is an ethereal place which may have made some people think of a heaven. Often, we find teachers here, with important messages for the seeker or sick individual. Journeys to the Upper World often take place in contact with spirit guides, ancestors, and sentient spirits.

While the shaman may visit and collect information from upper, lower, and middle worlds, they must understand the magnificence of the worlds they are visiting and what they are collecting from each for healing. Above all, they must not confuse or misapply what it is they have collected during a ritual.

Different methods are used to induce trances cross-culturally. These methods can require excessive physical movement, including meditation, shamanic drumming, and dancing, but may also involve sleep deprivation, fasting, sleep, and psychoactive drugs. These types of behaviours are not haphazard; if sleep deprivation is present, fasting and social isolation are often also

---

[151] themystica.com, AlteredStatesofConsciousness.

present, such as when a young person goes alone into the forest on a quest for a guardian spirit. Moreover, these types of induction methods rarely are associated with possession trance.[152]

If sleeping is the method of inducing a trance, usually it does not involve possession, such as a soul journey. Possession trances, on the other hand, are associated with subsequent amnesia, convulsions, and spontaneous onset of trances.[153]

Trance and other altered states of consciousness are strongly associated with healing practices of shamans, who are a subset of magico-religious healers. Among shamans, trances are usually induced by mechanisms such as singing, chanting, drumming, or dancing, after which the shaman in training or practice collapses and becomes unconscious and has intense visual experiences. These experiences presumably induce a state of relaxation that replaces fast brain activity in the front areas of the brain with slow wave activity representing more emotional information.[154]

Shamanic music[155] is music played either by actual shamans as part of their rituals, or by people who, whilst not themselves shamans, wish to evoke the cultural background of shamanism in some way. So shamanic music includes both music used as part of shamans' rituals and music that refers to, or draws on, this.

In shamanism the shaman has a more active musical role than the medium in spirit possession. Although shamans use singing, drumming, and sometimes other instruments, a shamanic ritual is not a musical performance in the normal sense, and the music is directed more to spirits than to an audience and this shapes its musical dimension. A shaman uses various ways of making sounds to which different ritual purposes are ascribed. Of particular importance are the shaman's song and the shaman's drumming.

Siberian music groups drawing on knowledge of shamanic culture have emerged. In the West, shamanism has served as an imagined background to music meant to alter a listener's state of mind.

Korea and Tibet are two cultures where the music of shamanic ritual has interacted closely with other traditions.

How ritual forms the musical expression:

1. A shamanic ritual performance is, above all, a series of actions and not a series of musical sounds.

2. The intention of the shaman's actions and music is directed inwards towards his or her visualization of the spirit world and communicating with the spirits, and not outward to any listeners who might be present.

3. Success of the ritual and its purpose in healing are very clearly defined and are very different from, and ignores, any thought of performing entertainment.

---

[152] themystica.com, AlteredStatesofConsciousness.
[153] themystica.com, AlteredStatesofConsciousness.
[154] https://hraf.yale.edu, AlteredStatesofConsciousness.
[155] Wikipedia, Shamanicmusic.

4. Theatrical elements that have been added to impress an audience are of a type to make contact with the spirits seem more real. They do not have a bearing on the performer's musical virtuosity. The added theatrical elements do not change the fundamental core of the shaman's ritual connection with the spirits must, and does, remain unchanged.

5. The overarching pace and tone and style of the music and singing proceed at the pace of the spirits being communicated and the essential healing process being carried out. Theatrical considerations are ignored.

6. The rhythmic dimension of the music of shamans' rituals has been connected to the idea of both incorporating the rhythms of nature and magically rearticulating them.

Shamans in Tibet, Mongolia, and Northern Siberia are often skilled at working with plants and sacred herbs in order to provide or prescribe plant-based medicines for the recipient. Drumming, singing and dance are the usual ways for a shaman to induce an altered state of consciousness or trance state where they can journey to the spirit world and interact with their helping spirits and conduct spiritual healing. From time to time and depending on the shaman's lineage and method of practice, plants that have a psychoactive substance may be used to induce a trance.

When using psychoactive substances, the shaman must be very careful because the substance is changing their state of consciousness and they do not have any control over the intensity, duration and any residue left in their system once ingested. This is very different from a shaman using drumming, song, and dance where no drug is used. The shaman actively enters the spirit world and works with their helping spirits to perform their healing activity. They negotiate with her or his own helper spirit and then with other spirits as necessary, and move between different territories of the upper middle and lower spirit worlds.
Whilst in the spirit world, the shaman must use considerable mental and spiritual awareness, they must be active and be able to take the initiative. A drug will impede their abilities and may make them susceptible to attack and damage by evil and malevolent spirits.

In contrast, a medium is passive and possessed by the spirit or god; they are connected to and this results in a different musical style. Possession music is typically long in duration, mesmeric, loud and intense, with climaxes of rhythmic intensity and volume to which the medium has learned to respond by entering a trance state: the music is not played by the medium but by one or more musicians.[156]

In shamanism, the music is played by the shaman; the words in the song confirm the shaman's power, and are actively used by the shaman to modulate movements and changes of state as part of an active journey within the spirit world. In both cases, the connection between music and an altered state of mind depends on both psychoacoustic and cultural factors, and music cannot be said to cause' trance states.

It has been suggested that the drumming and singing of the shaman constitute a system of sounds. This would suggest a system of semiotics shared between the shaman and the surrounding community. However, research suggests that if such a language exists, it is only understood by the shaman, other shamans, and the spirits being contacted, not the human community witnessing the ritual.

---

[156] Wikipedia, Shamanicmusic.

A shaman may use different sounds for different ritual purposes:

26.2. Shaman's Drum

The single-headed frame drum is widely used in shamanic rituals, often with metallic ritual objects dangling inside, held by an interior wooden cross-piece, and played with a special beater that may also itself be a rattle.

The drum and rattle are made of specially chosen and consecrated materials. Wood from a tree felled by lightning, the skin from a particular animal, a drum beater that may also be a ritual rattle in it is own right. Finally, enlivened by the shaman's helping spirits. Enlivening means the drum will contain a particular spirit with whom the shaman maintains a relationship and the spirit will play a part in any rituals performed using it.

A number of theories have been advanced to explain the importance of percussion in ritual music in general. One line of explanation is psychoacoustic, whereby the tempo of the drum enables the shaman to enter the desired brain wave state, which corresponds to the number of beats per second of the drum.[157]

In shamanism, a portable drum is better suited, as it can be played easily and during rituals where the shaman must drum and dance. For this reason, the drumming is not restricted to regular tempo but may speed up and slow down with irregular accents. In some regions, the skin of a shaman's drum should be cut after his/her death. This allows the spirit enlivening the drum to be released, and so that no other shaman, or ordinary person, can use the drum to connect with the spirit world using it.

The drumbeat acts like a tether for the journeyer to hold onto as they travel and it keeps them grounded. Let's use the example of a kite. The kite is the person who is journeying. The string is the sound of the drum. Live drumming induces a deeper ASC, as it also usually involves dance and physical motion.

26.3. Bon Shamanic Music and Buddhism

Bon predates Tibetan Buddhism. When Buddhism arrived in approximately the eighth century AD, both religions began competing with each other, but they also incorporated many of each other's practices. Bön shaman's drum, but now placed on a pole, became part of Tibetan Buddhist ritual music ensembles. The Shang—a kind of bell symbol—became incorporated in Buddhist rituals.[158] It was formerly only used by shamans to clear away negative energy before shamanic rituals.[159]

The Shang bell is not the same as the Tibetan Buddhist Tingsha bell.

The practice of giving a sonorous identity to deities, of calling them and sending them back by sounds, may well have entered Tibetan Buddhist ritual from Bön tradition.[160]

26.4. Bells and Cymbals

---

[157] Wikipedia, Shamanicmusic.
[158] https://garudashop.com/collections/bonpo-shang-bell, BonpoShangBell|TraditionalTibetaninstrument.
[159] Wikipedia, Shamanicmusic.
[160] Wikipedia, Shamanicmusic.

Bells and symbols are used in conjunction with the drum as part of the ritual and are essential to the safety of the shaman as they enter an altered state of consciousness and exist in the spirit world.

Bells and symbols are used for purifying the ritual space. This is because a ritual involving contact with the spirits is always potentially dangerous, and one of the dangers is that of pollution.

Bells and cymbals may be attached to the shamans' costume, the drum and drum better or rattle they are using to ensure safety and purification of all clothing and ensure the sound created by the shaman is purified. Sound can also be used as a healing power, conceived as a way of directing spiritual energy from the shaman into an afflicted person. In Tuva, sick persons are said to have been healed by the sound of a stringed instrument made from a tree struck by lightning.[161]

26.5. Dreams

Dreaming, a nearly universal channel into an altered state of consciousness, is much more widely available than lengthy rituals with music and dance or the use of drugs.

A shaman will use their own dreams and the dreams of the person they are to heal as part of the divination and diagnosis process to determine how to proceed. At the end of the ritual and after a period of healing, use of dreams by the Shaman can confirm the success of the rituals and healing or whether further intervention is required.

26.6. Other Thoughts

Other cultures say that it is the patient that must achieve the trance, not the shaman. In Islamic North Africa and the Arabian Peninsula, the Zar ritual is used to rid negative spirits from the body of the patient, but the leader of the ceremony does not go into trance; it is the patient that must achieve ecstasy for healing to occur. In A'isha Ali's video of "Dances of Egypt", she shows a Zar ceremony, and music and dance are essential for the patient to achieve a trance. While there is definitely a leader of the ceremony, a shamanic figure, she is merely the orchestrator/mediator of the event, not the central figure. [162]

---

[161] Wikipedia, Shamanicmusic.
[162] KatyaFaris.com, AlteredStatesofConsciousnessandHealinginIndigenousRituals-KatyaFaris.

27. Tibetan Book of the Dead.

Bardo—Tibetan—Bar do thos grol translates as: [163]

1. Bardo "intermediate state," "transitional state," "in between states," "liminal state," which is synonymous with the Sanskrit antarabhāva. Valdez: "Used loosely, the term 'Bardo' refers to the state of existence intermediate between two lives on earth." Valdez: "[The] concept arose soon after the Buddha's passing, with a number of earlier Buddhist groups accepting the existence of such an intermediate state, while other schools rejected it."

2. Thos grol: "liberation," which is synonymous with the Sanskrit word bodhi, "awakening," "understanding," "enlightenment," and synonymous with the term nirvana, "blowing out," "extinction," "the extinction of illusion."

3. In Tibetan Buddhism, Bardo is the central theme of the Bardo Thodol literally Liberation Through Hearing During the Intermediate State, or the Tibetan Book of the Dead

27.2. Origins.

In Tibetan tradition, the Bardo Thodol, Liberation Through Hearing During the Intermediate State — The Tibetan Book of the Dead was composed in the 8th century by Padmasambhava, written down by his primary student, Yeshe Tsogyal, buried in the Gampo hills in central Tibet and subsequently discovered by a Tibetan terton[164], Karma Lingpa, in the 14th century.[165]

In some schools of Buddhism, Bardo, antarabhava, or chuu is an intermediate, transitional, or liminal state between death and rebirth—reincarnation. Reincarnation into another life, as a different being, is the philosophical or religious concept that the non-physical essence of a living being starts a new life in a different physical form or body after biological death. It is also called rebirth or transmigration.[166]

Bardo or Bardo Thodol is a concept which arose soon after the Buddha's passing, with a number of earlier Buddhist groups accepting the existence of such an intermediate state, while other schools rejected it.

In Tibetan Buddhism, Bardo is the central theme of the Bardo Thodol[167]; literally Liberation Through Hearing During the Intermediate State, in the west, Bardo Thodol is known as the Tibetan Book of the Dead.[168] The Tibetan Book of the Dead is a Lamest book of counsel, probably influenced by Bon shamanism. The Tibetan text is intended to guide one through the experiences consciousness has after death, in the Bardo, the interval between death and the next rebirth. The text also includes chapters on the signs of death and rituals to undertake when death is closing in or has taken place.

---

[163] Wikipedia, BardoThodol.
[164] Wikipedia, Terton.
[165] http://donlehmanjr.com/, TheTibetanBookoftheDead.pdf.
[166] Wikipedia, Reincarnation.
[167] Britannica, BardoThödolTibetanBuddhisttext.
[168] Wikipedia, Bardo.

One common error with the Tibetan Book of the dead is that it is not whispered into the dying person's ear! In Tibetan Buddhist practice, the Tibetan Book of the Dead is used during life by those who want to learn to visualize what will come after death.

After physical death, it is the tribal shaman, a psychopomp or soul-guide who accompanies the soul of the dead person on their difficult path during the forty-nine days of the intermediate state between death and rebirth.[169]

According to Tibetan tradition, after death and before one's next birth, when one's consciousness is not connected with a physical body, one experiences a variety of phenomena. These usually follow a particular sequence of degeneration from just after death, the clearest experiences of reality of which one is spiritually capable, and then proceeding to terrifying hallucinations that arise from the impulses of one's previous unskillful actions. For the prepared and appropriately trained individuals, the Bardo offers a state of great opportunity for liberation, since transcendental insight may arise with the direct experience of reality; for others, it can become a place of danger, as the karmically created hallucinations can impel one into a less than desirable rebirth.[170]

Symbolically, Bardo describes times when our usual way of life becomes suspended, as, for example, during a period of illness or during a meditation retreat. Such times can prove fruitful for spiritual progress because external constraints diminish. However, they can also present challenges because our less skillful impulses may come to the foreground, just as in the sidpa Bardo.

The concept of antarabhava,[171] an intervening state between death and rebirth, was brought into Buddhism from the Vedic-Upanishadic philosophical tradition, which later developed into Hinduism.

From the records of early Buddhist schools, it appears that at least six different groups accepted the notion of an intermediate existence: antarabhava, namely, the Sarvastivada, Darstantika, Vatsiputriyas, Sammitiya, Purvasaila, and late Mahisasaka. The first four of these are closely related schools. Opposing them was the Mahasamghika, early Mahisasaka, Theravada, Vibhajyavada and the Sariputra Abhidharma.

To the shaman, the world has three parts: the sky and heavens, earth, and the lower regions, or realms.

Each has its own distinctive spirits, many of which influence the world of humans, including souls in the process of crossing over. The upper gods (steng lha) live in the atmosphere and sky. In the middle realm tsen (bar btsan) inhabit the earth, in the lower realm is the home of yoklu (g.yog klu), most notably snake-bodied beings called Lu (klu Naga), which live at the bottom of lakes, rivers, and wells and are reported to hoard vast stores of treasure. As all things have a spirit, the spirits residing in rocks and trees are called nyen (gnyan); they are often malicious, and Tibetans associate them with sickness and death.

Lu is believed to bring leprosy, and so it is important to keep them away from human habitations. Sadak (sa bdag, "lords of the earth") are beings that live under the ground and are connected with

---

[169] University of California Press eBook Collection, TheSpiritualQuest, (1982 - 2004).
[170] Wikipedia, Bardo.
[171] https://www.wisdomlib.org, Antarabhava,Antarābhavadefinitions.

agriculture. Tsen are spirits that live in the atmosphere, and are believed to shoot arrows at humans who disturb them. These cause illness and death. Tsen appears as demonic figures with red skin, wearing helmets and riding over the mountains in red horses. Du (bdud, mara) were apparently originally atmospheric spirits, but they came to be associated with the Buddhist demons called mara, which are led by their king (also named Mara), whose primary goal is to lead sentient beings into ignorance, thus perpetuating the vicious cycle of samsara.

After death, the shaman undertakes a journey to the intermediate world and with the help of their helping spirits seek out the soul of the deceased and guide and encourages it to cross over fully, especially if the wandering soul has been affecting the lives of living relatives or otherwise causing problems. Or has been interacting with the spirits in the intermediate realm. During the ritual, blocked energies are released, transformed, and healed so that the soul can receive higher spiritual knowledge when they actually make the crossing.

The shaman may also be asked to help souls and spirits cross over who had no connection to the living. For some reason the soul has not crossed over and connected themselves to a living person. That connection causes illness. Usually, the sick individual or their family members will ask a shaman to carry out a divination ceremony where the shaman will determine what is causing the illness. The next step is to act on the reason that has been uncovered. If it is a spirit that has connected themselves to the living, the shaman will perform another ceremony to help it detach and cross over.

In the process, the shaman may undertake spiritual battles, confront evil or dark spirits and souls in order to help a sick individual or to help the spirt affecting them to cross over. The upper, middle or intermediate, and lower realms are also inhabited by the spirits of ancestors [of the sick person] and the shaman must understand them, and may persuade them to help a soul in its current physical incarnation.

The antagonism that often exists between scientifically trained and those professing particular religions can be considerable there is often little study of each other's accounts of religious and psychic phenomena, so books like those mentioned are often not known outside a narrow circle of experts or academic authorities. Yet it is worth noting that Carol Zaleski's[172] book has already spawned a whole academic field of research into the phenomenology of "otherworldly realities"— there have been several international conferences to date—while Sogyal's[173] book is now used worldwide to help people who are nearing death prepare for their passing over. [174]

In Buddhism Some of the earliest references, we have the "intermediate existence" are found in the Sarvastivadin text the Mahavibhasa. For instance, the Mahavibhasa indicates a "basic existence," an "intermediate existence," a "birth existence" and "death existence."

The intermediate being who makes the passage in this way from one existence to the next is formed, like every living being, of the five aggregate skandhas[175]. Existence is demonstrated by the fact that it cannot have any discontinuity in time and space between the place and moment of death and those of rebirth, and therefore it must be that the two existences belonging to the same series are linked in time and space by an intermediate stage. The intermediate being is the Gandharva, the presence of which is as necessary at conception as the fecundity and union of the

---

[172] Wikipedia, CarolZaleski.
[173] Wikipedia, SogyalRinpoche.
[174] Dr. Roger J. Woolger, BeyondDeath-TransitionandtheAfterlife.
[175] Wikipedia, Skandha.

parents. Furthermore, the Antaraparinirvayin is an Anagamin who obtains parinirvana during the intermediary existence. As for the heinous criminally guilty of one of the five crimes without interval (Anantara), he passes in quite the same way by an intermediate existence at the end of which he is reborn, necessarily in hell.[176]

What is an intermediate being and an intermediate existence? Intermediate existence, which inserts itself between existence at death and existence at birth, not having arrived at the location where it should go, cannot be said to be born. Between death—that is, the five skandhas of the moment of death—and arising—that is, the five skandhas of the moment of rebirth—there is found an existence—a "body" of five skandhas—that goes to the place of rebirth. This existence between two realms of rebirth (gati) is called intermediate existence. The skandhas are referred to as heaps because they're merely collections of parts without any central core.

Skandha	Description
Form	Your physical body—traditionally, these are listed as the eyes, ears, nose, tongue, body, and mind.
Feeling	The sensations you experience in your body, including all pain and pleasure.
Perception	You have sense organs, and each of them has objects. Put them together—eye and light, nose and smell, etc.—and you have perception.
Mental	All your concepts and thoughts, from the most mundane to the most grandiose.
Consciousness	Simply put, this is your awareness of the previous skandhas.

---

[176] Wikipedia, Bardo.

28. Six Bardo States

These are transitional states within the 49-day period the soul of the deceased is transitioning to their next life, their rebirth. But to be precise, Bardo refers to that state in which we have lost our old reality and it is no longer available to us.

What makes death and impermanence so painful is our idea of the strict dichotomy between existence and nonexistence. Knowing something beyond that dualism is paramount. At the moment of death, instead of being caught between the ideas of existence and nonexistence, instead of this crisis of having everything that matters to us taken away all at once, something else can open up entirely; we shift our attention to the nucleus of being, to present itself and experiencing itself.[177]

Without some way of managing this experience, this unsettling discontinuity punctuated by occasional disruptions to the very idea of our being, we never know if we are going to show up in the next moment as a Buddha or as a demon. We're like gods one moment, tasting the fruit of the kingdom, and hungry ghosts the next, not even able to swallow it. How confusing—and how fantastic! This confusion is the raw material of wisdom. Our path is to find a presence in each of these experiences. In the case of the Bardo, when presence is the only real thing left, if we are searching for security instead, wisdom can be elusive. It's no wonder that religion becomes so poignant during times of crisis; suddenly, presence is all we are. Everything else recedes except what is right in front of us. Recognizing this opens up the potential to experience life with awareness of impermanence and the presence it illuminates.[178]

- Rupture: There is a total rupture in our who-I-am, and we are forced to undergo a great and difficult transformation.

This is the Vajrayana awareness of successive deaths and rebirths, and it is the first essential point to understand: rupture. The more we learn to recognize this sense of disruption, the more willing and able to let go of this notion of an inherent reality and allow that precious pot to slip out of our hands. Rupture takes place all the time, day to day and moment to moment; in fact, as soon as we see our life in terms of these successive deaths and rebirths, we dissolve the very idea of a solid self-grasping onto an inherently real life. We start to see how conditional who-I-am-ness really is and how even that does not provide reliable ground upon which to stand.

- Emptying the Contrived Self:

This is shunyata[179], which gets translated in various ways, most commonly as "emptiness," but there is no real correlation in our language, no single word or idea that can cover this ground of disrupted reality. Because "emptiness" in English has negative connotations, shunyata is sometimes translated as "voidness," "open spaciousness," and even "boundlessness"; Nyingmas[180] such as Longchenpa explained emptiness in positive terms inextricably associated with presence, clarity, and compassion. But in the context of death and birth, shunyata refers to a

---

[177] Lionsroar.com, TheFourPointsofLettingGointheBardo.
[178] Lionsroar.com, TheFourPointsofLettingGointheBardo.
[179] www.rigpawiki.org, Emptiness.
[180] www.rigpawiki.org, NyingmaBuddhism.

direct experience of disruption felt at the core of our being when there is no longer any use manufacturing artificial security.[181]

- Recognition that our experience is based on dynamic, responsive presence.

Our goal is to learn to relax and how to do so and fall into the inherent peacefulness of not knowing what comes next. When we do—and to the extent that we do—everything changes. We are no longer slaves to primordial anxiety.

Experiencing a loss can be freeing. When we are free of all our psychological heaviness and the accumulated weight of our usual momentum, we have an opportunity to know the raw presence that remains. To be a Buddhist is to dedicate our lives to abiding in that impermanent, empty, visceral presence. We can bear with greater ease those losses that we know we will inevitably face because we identify with the thread of wakefulness that we meet in all of them. And then perhaps, when death draws near, we can relax with ease into the ground of being as we shed this skin, finally let go of this body, and experience liberation—undefended being in groundless space.[182]

Please See—Bardo, Wikipedia—https://en.wikipedia.org/wiki/Bardo

1. Kyenay Bardo—Skye gnas bar do is the first Bardo of birth and life. This Bardo commences from conception until the last breath when the mind stream withdraws from the body.

2. Milam Bardo—rmi lam bar do is the second Bardo of the dream state. The Milam Bardo is a subset of the first Bardo. Dream Yoga develops practices to integrate the dream state into Buddhist sadhana.

3. Samten Bardo—bsam gtan bar do is the third Bardo of meditation. This Bardo is generally only experienced by meditators, though individuals may have spontaneous experience of it. Samten Bardo is a subset of the Shinay Bardo.

4. Chikhai Bardo—'chi kha'i bar do is the fourth Bardo of the moment of death. According to tradition, this Bardo is held to commence when the outer and inner signs presage that the onset of death is nigh, and continues through the dissolution or transmutation of the Mahabhuta until the external and internal breath has completed.

    This is the first of three intermediate states between lives in the Tibetan Book of the dead.

5. Chonyid Bardo—chos nyid bar do is the fifth Bardo of the luminosity of true nature, which commences after the final "inner breath" Sanskrit: prana, Vayu; Tibetan: rlung. It is within this Bardo that visions and auditory phenomena occur. In the Dzogchen teachings, these are known as the spontaneously manifesting Thodgal Tibetan: thod-rgyal visions.

---

[181] Lionsroar.com, TheFourPointsofLettingGointheBardo.
[182] Lionsroar.com, TheFourPointsofLettingGointheBardo.

Concomitant to these visions, there is a welling of profound peace and pristine awareness. Sentient beings who have not practised during their lived experience and/or who do not recognize the clear light Tibetan: OD gsal at the moment of death are usually deluded throughout the fifth Bardo of luminosity.

This is the second of three intermediate states between lives in the Tibetan Book of the dead.

6. Sidpa Bardo—srid pa bar do is the sixth Bardo of becoming or transmigration. This Bardo endures until the inner breath commences in the new transmigrating form determined by the "karmic seeds" within the storehouse consciousness.

This is the third of three intermediate states between lives in the Tibetan Book of the dead.

28.4. Bardo Thodol and additional states

C. G. Jung's[183] psychological commentary on the Tibetan Book of the Dead first appeared in an English translation by R. F. C. Hull in the third revised and expanded Evans-Wentz edition of The Tibetan Book of the Dead. The commentary also appears in the Collected Works. Jung applied his extensive knowledge of eastern religion to craft a commentary specifically aimed at a western audience unfamiliar with eastern religious tradition in general and Tibetan Buddhism specifically.[184]

He does not attempt to directly correlate the content of the Bardo Thodol with rituals or dogma found in occidental religion, but rather highlights karmic phenomena described on the Bardo plane and shows how they parallel unconscious contents both personal and collective encountered in the west, particularly in the context of analytical psychology.[185]

Jung's comments should be taken strictly within the realm of psychology, and not that of theology or metaphysics. Indeed, he repeatedly warns of the dangers for western man in the wholesale adoption of eastern religious traditions, such as yoga.[186]

Bardo Thodol—Tibetan Book of the Dead recognizes three other states.[187]

1. "Life," or ordinary waking consciousness;

2. "Dhyana" (meditation);

   In the oldest texts of Buddhism, dhyāna (Sanskrit) or jhāna (Pali) is the training of the mind, commonly translated as meditation, to withdraw the mind from the automatic responses to sense impressions, leading to a "state of perfect equanimity and awareness (upekkhā-sati-parisuddhi)." Dhyana may have been the core practice of pre-sectarian Buddhism, in

---

[183] Wikipedia, CarlJung.
[184] Wikipedia, BardoThodol.
[185] Wikipedia, BardoThodol.
[186] Wikipedia, BardoThodol.
[187] Wikipedia, BardoThodol.

combination with several related practices, which together lead to perfected mindfulness and detachment, and are fully realized with the practice of dhyana.

3. "Dream," the dream state during normal sleep. Places in Tibet

29. Sacred Places

29.1. Mount Kailash

The mountain is located near Lake Manasarovar and Lake Rakshastal, close to the source of some of the longest Asian rivers: the Indus, Sutlej, Brahmaputra, and Karnali, also known as Ghaghara (a tributary of the Ganges) in India.[188]

A great mass of black rock soaring to over 22,000 feet, Mt. Kailash has the unique distinction of being the world's most venerated holy place at the same time that it is the least visited. The supremely sacred site of four religions and billions of people, Mt. Kailash is seen by no more than a few thousand pilgrims each year. This curious fact is explained by the mountain's remote location in far western Tibet. No planes, trains, or buses journey anywhere near the region and even with rugged overland vehicles, the journey still requires weeks of difficult, often dangerous travel. The weather, always cold, can be unexpectedly treacherous and pilgrims must carry all the supplies they will need for the entire journey.[189]

The cosmologies and origin myths of each of these religions speak of Mt. Kailash as the mythical Mt. Meru, the Axis Mundi, the centre, and the birth place of the entire world. The mountain was already legendary before the great Hindu epics, the Ramayana and the Mahabharata, were written. Indeed, Kailash is so deeply embedded in the myths of ancient Asia that it was perhaps a sacred place of another era, another civilization, now long gone and forgotten.

For Tibetans, pilgrimage refers to the journey from ignorance to enlightenment, from self-centredness and materialistic preoccupations to a deep sense of the relativity and interconnectedness of all life. The Tibetan word for pilgrimage, neykhor, means "to circle around a sacred place," for the goal of pilgrimage is less to reach a particular destination than to transcend through inspired travel the attachments and habits of inattention that restrict awareness of a larger reality.[190]

---

[188] Wikipedia, MountKailash.
[189] Sacredsites.com, WorldPilgrimigaeguide.
[190] Sacredsites.com, WorldPilgrimigaeguide.

30. Bon

Bon, a religion native to Tibet, maintains that the entire mystical region and Kailash, which they call the "nine-story Swastika Mountain," are the axis mundi, Tagzig Olmo Lung Ring.

The great Vajrayana sage, Milarepa, seeking to establish Buddhism in Tibet, engaged in a magical battle with the Bon shaman, Naro-Bon-Chung to win the heart of the Tibetan people. It is said they battled for many days with no clear victor. The final and decisive stage of the battle was a race to the top of Mount Kailash, the same mountain associated with Shiva. Milarepa won, but in a gesture of generosity and compassion tossed a snowball to Naro-Bon-Chung. A gesture understood to symbolize the syncretic integration of the new dispensation of Buddhism with the old shamanic Bon tradition. There could hardly be a more perfect expression of the Archangel Zadkiel's righteous compassion and sense of justice that transcends ego.[191]

30.1. Hindus

Hindus believe Mt. Kailash to be the abode of Lord Shiva. Like many of the Hindu gods, Shiva is a character of apparent contradictions. He at once the Lord of Yoga and therefore the ultimate renunciate ascetic, yet he is also the divine master of Tantra, the esoteric science that regards sexual union as the most perfect path to spiritual enlightenment. According to legend, immortal Shiva lives atop Kailash, where he spends his time practising yogic austerities, making joyous love with his divine consort, Parvati, and smoking ganja, the sacred herb known in the west as marijuana. Hindus do not interpret Shiva's behaviours as contradictory, however, but rather see in him a deity who has wisely integrated the extremes of human nature and thus transcended attachment to any particular, and limited, way of being. For a Hindu, to make the arduous pilgrimage to Kailash and have the darshan (divine view) of Shiva's abode is to obtain release from the clutches of ignorance and delusion.[192]

30.2. Jains

Mt. Kailash is sacred to other religions as well. The Jains call the mountain Astapada and believe it to be the place where Rishaba, the first of the twenty-four Tirthankaras, attained liberation. Followers of Bon, Tibet's pre-Buddhist, shamanistic religion, call the mountain Tise and believe it to be the seat of the Sky Goddess Sipaimen. Additionally, Bon myths regard Tise as the sight of a legendary 12th-century battle of sorcery between the Buddhist sage Milarepa and the Bon shaman Naro Bon-Chung. Milarepa's defeat of the shaman displaced Bon as the primary religion of Tibet, firmly establishing Buddhism in its place. While the Buddha is believed to have magically visited Kailash in the fifth century BC, the religion of Buddhism only entered Tibet, via Nepal and India, in the seventh century AD. Tibetan Buddhists call the mountain Kang Rimpoche, the "Precious One of Glacial Snow," and regard it as the dwelling place of Demchog (also known as Chakrasamvara) and his consort, Dorje Phagmo. Three hills rising near Kang Rimpoche are believed to be the homes of the Bodhisattvas Manjushri, Vajrapani, and Avalokiteshvara.

After the difficult journey getting to Mt. Kailash, they are confronted by the arduous task of circumambulating the sacred peak. This walking around the mountain (clockwise for the Buddhists, counter-clockwise for Bon adherents) is known as a Kora, or Parikrama, and normally takes three days.

---

[191] wingsofchaos.com, PrologueforZadkiel.
[192] Sacredsites.com, WorldPilgrimigaeguide.

In hopes of gaining extra merit or psychic powers, however, some pilgrims will vary the tempo of their movement. A hardy few, practising a secret breathing technique known as Lung-gom, will power themselves around the mountain in only one day. Others will take two to three weeks for the kora by making full-body prostration the entire way. It is believed that a pilgrim who completes 108 journeys around the mountain is assured enlightenment. Most pilgrims to Kailash will also take a short plunge in the nearby, highly sacred (and very cold) Lake Manosaravar. The word "manas" means mind or consciousness; the name Manosaravar means Lake of Consciousness and Enlightenment. Adjacent to Manosaravar is Rakas Tal or Rakshas, the Lake of Demons. Pilgrimage to this great sacred mountain and these two magical lakes is a life-changing experience and an opportunity to view some of the most magical scenery on the entire planet.

30.3. Potala Palace:

The Potala Palace is a dzong fortress in the city of Lhasa, in China's Tibet Autonomous Region. It was the winter palace of the Dalai Lamas from 1649 to 1959, has been a museum since then, and has been a World Heritage Site since 1994. [193]

The site on which the Potala Palace rises is built over a palace erected by Songtsen Gampo on the Red Hill. The Potala contains two chapels on its northwest corner that conserve parts of the original building. One is the Phakpa Lhakhang, the other the Chogyel Drupuk, a recessed cavern identified as Songtsen Gampo's meditation cave.

Lozang Gyatso, the Great Fifth Dalai Lama, started the construction of the modern Potala Palace in 1645 after one of his spiritual advisors, Konchog Chophel (died 1646), pointed out that the site was ideal as a seat of government, situated as it is between Drepung and Sera monasteries and the old city of Lhasa. The external structure was built in 3 years, while the interior, together with its furnishings, took 45 years to complete.

The Dalai Lama and his government moved into the Potrang Karpo ("White Palace") in 1649. Construction lasted until 1694, some twelve years after his death. The Potala was used as a winter palace by the Dalai Lama from that time. The Potrang Marpo ("Red Palace") was added between 1690 and 1694.

---

[193] Wikipedia, PotalaPalace.

30.4. Jokhang Temple

Jokhang Temple is a Buddhist temple.

The Jokhang was founded during the reign of King Songtsen Gampo. According to tradition, the temple was built for the king's two brides: Princess Wencheng of the Chinese Tang dynasty and Princess Bhrikuti of Nepal. Both are said to have brought important Buddhist statues and images from China and Nepal to Tibet, which were housed here, as part of their dowries. The oldest part of the temple was built in 652. Over the next 900 years, the temple was enlarged several times, with the last renovation done in 1610 by the Fifth Dalai Lama. Following the death of Gampo, the image in Ramcho Lake temple was moved to the Jokhang temple for security reasons. When King Tresang Detsen ruled from 755 to 797, the Buddha image of the Jokhang temple was hidden, as the king's minister was hostile to the spread of Buddhism in Tibet. During the late ninth and early tenth centuries, the Jokhang and Ramoche temples were said to have been used as stables. In 1049 Atisha, a renowned teacher of Buddhism from Bengal, taught in Jokhang.[194]

Tibetans viewed their country as a living entity controlled by srin ma (pronounced "sinma"), a wild demoness who opposed the propagation of Buddhism in the country. To thwart her evil intentions, King Songtsen Gampo, the first king of a unified Tibet, developed a plan to build twelve temples across the country. The temples were built in three stages. In the first stage, central Tibet was covered with four temples, known as the "four horns" (ru bzhi). Four more temples (mtha'dul) were built in the outer areas in the second stage; the last four, the yang'dul, were built on the country's frontiers. The Jokhang temple was finally built in the heart of the srin ma, ensuring her subjugation.[195]

30.5. Norbulingka:

In Tibetan, Norbulingka means "Treasure Garden." Or "Treasure Park." The word "Lingka" is commonly used in Tibet to define all horticultural parks in Lhasa and other cities. When the Cultural Revolution began in 1966, Norbulingka was renamed People's Park and opened to the public.[196]

Norbulingka Palace of the Dalai Lamas was built about 100 years after the Potala Palace was built on the Parkori peak, over a 36 hectares 89 acres land area. It was built a little away to the west of the Potala for the exclusive use by the Dalai Lama to stay in during the summer months. Tenzing Gyatso, the present 14th Dalai Lama, stayed here before he fled to India. The building of the palace and the park was undertaken by the 7th Dalai Lama from 1755. The Norbulingka Park and Summer Palace were completed in 1783 under Jampel Gyatso, the 8th Dalai Lama, on the outskirts of Lhasa. And became the summer residence during the reign of the Eighth Dalai Lama.[197]

---

[194] Wikipedia, Jokhang.
[195] Wikipedia, Jokhang.
[196] Wikipedia, Norbulingka.
[197] Wikipedia, Norbulingka.

30.6. Drepung Monastery

'Drepung Monastery, located at the foot of Mount Gephel, is one of the "great three" Gelug University gompas (monasteries) of Tibet. The other two are Ganden Monastery and Sera Monastery.[198]

Drepung is the largest of all Tibetan monasteries and is located on the Gambo Utse Mountain, five kilometres from the western suburb of Lhasa.

Drepung Monastery was founded in 1416 by Jamyang Choge Tashi Palden (1397–1449), one of Tsongkhapa's main disciples, and it was named after the sacred abode in South India of Shridhanyakataka. Drepung was the principal seat of the Gelugpa school and it retained the premier place among the four great Gelugpa monasteries. The Ganden Phodrang (dga' ldan pho brang) in Drepung was the residence of the Dalai Lamas until the Great Fifth Dalai Lama constructed the Potala. Drepung was known for the high standards of its academic study, and was called the Nalanda of Tibet, a reference to the great Buddhist monastic University of India. [199]

---

[198] Wikipedia, DrepungMonastery.
[199] Wikipedia, DrepungMonastery.

31. Bon Religion

Bon is an ancient shamanist religion. It is indigenous to the Himalayas and Central Asia. Especially the Tibetan region, the religion contains rituals, exorcisms, talismans, spells, incantations, drumming, sacrifices, a pantheon of gods good and evil spirits, and a cult of the dead or ancestor worship.

While there is almost no written tradition of the early pre-Buddhist indigenous religious practices in the region, Bon has a coherent and unified system of doctrines based on a vast literature, more than 1,000 years old.[200]

It is the main aboriginal religion of the ancient Qinghai-Tibetan Plateau. It is said to have originated in the fifth century B.C. with Shenrab Miwoche, the prince of the Zhang-zhung kingdom in western Tibet. This means it predates Buddhism, which arrived in the seventh century AD by a long way.

Around the first century A.D., the religion began to spread eastward until it became widely practised in the Tsang and Lhasa regions. Bon is still practised today. It embraces pantheism and believes that "everything has a soul." Bon deities include supernatural powers of mountains, rivers, lakes, seas, the sun, the moon, stars, wind, rain, thunder, lightning, birds, and beasts, as many as one can enumerate. These deities govern the birth, ageing, sickness, death, events, and fortunes of people, who cannot predict and control their own destinies because people have been created by the deities.[201]

Yungdrung Bon is the teaching of the Central Asian Buddha, Tonpa Shenrab Miwoche, who lived and preached in the heart of Tagzig, an ancient country located somewhere in the Pamir Mountains, possibly in modern-day Tajikistan and/or the surrounding Central Asian republics. The teachings of this Buddha were brought into and flourished in the land of Zhang Zhung, an empire or tribal confederation centred in western Tibet around Tise (Mount Kailash). It is from this heartland that Yungdrung Bon reached Tibet, initially a small vassal state of Zhang Zhung, which eventually overthrew its overlord in the sixth-eighth centuries AD. Yungdrung Bon is divided into two major parts: Causal and Fruitional. In a nutshell, Causal Bon is comprised of a vast body of rituals designed to improve worldly conditions and lessen hardships in this life and gradually guide the practitioner towards the higher teachings of Fruitional Bon, which ultimately lead to Buddhahood.[202]

When Tonpa Shenrab came to Tibet, which, according to the well-known 20th-century Buddhist scholar Gedun Chophel, he blessed Tibet and its people, sharing many teachings, ceremonies, and religious dances that are distinctly Bon in origin. The most important change he introduced was to eliminate animal sacrifice.

At that time, the local practice was to sacrifice animals in order to appease spirits responsible for causing sickness and misfortune. Tonpa Shenrab taught them they could offer red torma and white torma in place of animals. Torma is figures made mostly of flour and butter used in tantric

---

[200] Rubin Museum of Art, BonPressRelease.
[201] CATHOLICS AND SUPERSTITION IN TIBET BON RELIGION, BONRELIGION,CATHOLICSANDSUPERSTITIONINTibet.
[202] Ermakov, BOANDBON-ANCIENTSHAMANICTRADITIONSOFSIBERIAANDTIBETINTHEIRRELATIONTOTHETEACHINGSOFACENTRALASIANBUDDHA.

rituals or as offerings in Tibetan Buddhism. They may be dyed in different colours, often white or red for the main body. They are made in specific shapes based on their purpose, usually conical in form.[203] In this way, Tonpa Shenrab established the peaceful enlightened Yungdrung-Bon tradition.[204]

Bon is rooted in nature, recognizing its aliveness and spiritual dimension. Bonpos, as the practitioners are called, cultivate strong relationships with the spiritual dimension through rituals, symbolic offerings and prayers. They believe that there are many kinds of beings that can affect one in both positive and negative ways. By maintaining awareness of such possibilities, one can be proactive in working with the various spirits to eliminate obstacles as well as receiving help.[205]

Many Bonpo practices and meditations are unique, most especially the Bon Five Element practice.

In the Bon tradition, the universe is made up of five elements. In fact, our body is composed of five elements (earth, water, fire, wind, and space). These five are expressed within us through the interconnection of flesh, blood, heat, breath, and consciousness. They are connected to the five organs: liver, kidneys, spleen, lungs, and heart. Those organs are in turn, connected to the five poisons; attachment, jealousy, ignorance, pride, and anger. The five poisons can, in turn, be transformed into the five wisdom: emptiness, mirror-like wisdom, wisdom of equality, discriminating wisdom, and all-accomplishing wisdom. The transformation of the five poisons into the five wisdoms is the basis of spiritual practice. Each element has its own corresponding spiritual deity. All sentient beings are connected with their inner and their outer [environmental], as well as the natural form of each element. In this way, Bon developed distinctly.[206]

Prayer flags, prayer wheels, sky burials, festival devil dances, spirit traps and rubbing holy stones—things that are associated with Tibetan religion and Tibetan Buddhism—all evolved from Bon.[207]

When Buddhism became established in Tibet, Bonpos recognized many Buddhist traditions were wise and effective and began incorporating those that furthered their own path of self-realization. Bonpos also recognized that we are all capable of achieving our original, pure state through developing awareness, compassion, and wisdom.

Today, Bon includes shamanic methods like those described above, as well as a sutra path prescribing moral precepts, a Tantra path using the body and energy to improve health of body and mind, and a Dzogchen[208] path, which teaches how to improve health of body and mind, and how to achieve and abide in the natural, pure state of being.

In Bon, shamans dispel demons and appease the gods, and employ a number of mudras (ritual postures), mantras (sacred speech), yantras (sacred art) and secret initiation rites.[209]

---

[203] Wikipedia, Torma.
[204] buddhaweekly.com/, Iinterview-bon-teacher-chaphur-rinpoche-explains-bon-different-similar-five-buddhist-schools-tibet.
[205] Bon: Indigenous Shamanism of Tibet, Bon-IndigenousShamanismofTibet.
[206] buddhaweekly.com/, Iinterview-bon-teacher-chaphur-rinpoche-explains-bon-different-similar-five-buddhist-schools-tibet.
[207]
[208] Wikipedia, Dzogchen.
[209] BON RELIGION, BONRELIGION,CATHOLICSANDSUPERSTITIONINTibet.

Modern Bon religion, known as Yungdrung-Bon, and Buddhism are very similar. They embrace many of the same practices and rituals, except they have different names or slight variations. Bonpo pilgrims, for example, circumambulate monuments and mountains and turn prayer wheels counterclockwise rather than clockwise as Buddhists do. They recite the Bon mantra "om matri muye sale du" rather than the Buddhist mantra "om Mani padem hum." The concepts of karma and rebirth and the six states of existence are featured prominently in Bon as they are in Buddhism. The word Bon sometimes carries with it the same meaning as dharma.

Bon is an ancient religion and philosophy that remains very much alive today. There are Bon monasteries in Tibet and India and many lamas and lay people practise both Buddhism and Bon equally.

Modern Bon is so similar to Buddhism that the Dalai Lama has accepted it as one of the five schools of Tibetan Buddhism.[210]

31.1. Primary Differences Between Buddhism and Bon

Many of the most significant differences are listed below in bullet form: [211]

- A counter-clockwise circumambulation and eight-syllable mantra instead of six.
- Karma is not as important in Bon; events are occasionally explained by acts of deities and spirits and such.
- Feminine deities play a bigger role, especially in cosmogony.
- Interestingly, however, the relationship between nuns and monks, and the treatment of the former overall, are less progressive than in Buddhist
- Clans remain important, and mitigate the adoption of the incarnate lama strategy.
- Bon rituals established in the canon.
- During the propagation of Bon, temples and stupas were built, but not monasteries, and the propagation was carried out by women and children nearly as much as by men.
- Marriage rituals are more prominent

31.2. Shamanism and Animism

Bon is both a shamanist and an animistic[212] religion.

Shamans have visions and perform various deeds during a trance and it is believed they have the power to control spirits in the body. They may leave normal existence and travel or fly to other

---

[210] BON RELIGION, BONRELIGION,CATHOLICSANDSUPERSTITIONINTibet.
[211] Tibetan Renaissance Seminar, BonBackgroundResearchfromtheTibetanRenaissanceSeminar.
[212] Wikipedia, Animism.

worlds. Manchu-Tungus nomads of Siberia and northern Chinese language, Shaman means "agitated or frenzied people."

Shaman is bridges between their communities and the spiritual world. During trances, which are induced during a ritual, shamans seek spirits to help cure illnesses, bring about good weather, predict the future, or communicate with deceased ancestors.

Animism attributes a distinct spiritual essence or soul to plants, inanimate objects, and natural phenomena. It is a belief in a supernatural power that organizes and animates the material universe and that ancestors watch over the living from the spirit world.

There are places on earth where sacred power is concentrated. Those places are held sacred and where communication with the spirit world takes place.

32. Shamanism: Rituals and Spirituality

Shamanism is universal and not bound by social or cultural conditions. It is the most ancient and most enduring spiritual tradition known to humanity. Shamanism predates and constitutes the foundation of all known religions or religious philosophies.[213]

In the Shaman's world view, spirits and demons inhabit everything around us. Every part of the natural environment is alive with different types of sentient forces. Literally, the world is alive, in the mountains, trees, rivers and lakes, rocks, fields, the sky, and the earth. There are supernatural spirits and souls. Added to this, each region has its own native spiritual beings, and people living in those areas are powerfully aware of their presence. In order to stay in the spirit's good graces, offerings are made, rituals performed and sometimes people will refrain from particular places to avoid the more dangerous forces.

The focus of Buddhist teaching and practice is centred on commonplace goals; seeking advice from shamans whose function is to contact spirits, to predict their influences on people's lives, and to perform rituals that either overcome harmful influences or otherwise ask for their help makes sense. Making such a request and receiving a shaman's aid are intended to give people a measure of control over their unpredictable lives and surroundings.

Rituals conducted today have changed greatly from those of previous centuries. This is not to say they are any less effective today; they are. But the style and form of them from previous centuries have changed. Comparing rituals and practices from previous generations or those performed centuries ago to today does not make sense.

When Tonpa Shenrab came to Tibet, which, according to the well-known 20th-century Buddhist scholar Gedun Chophel, he blessed Tibet and its people, sharing many teachings, ceremonies, and religious dances that are distinctly Bon in origin. The most important change he introduced was to eliminate animal sacrifices. At that time, the local practice was to sacrifice animals in order to appease spirits responsible for causing sickness and misfortune. Tonpa Shenrab taught them they could offer red torma and white torma in place of animals. Torma are figures made mostly of flour and butter used in tantric rituals or as offerings in Tibetan Buddhism. They may be dyed in different colours, often with white or red for the main body of the torma. They are made in specific shapes based on their purpose, usually conical in form.[214] In this way, Tonpa Shenrab established the peaceful enlightened Yungdrung-Bon tradition.[215]

The Shaman is contemporary to the world they live in. They wear clothes and use tools and aids suitable to the society and expectations of their clients. To bring "bear" energy to his or her client, the shaman may wear something to connect with that animal or spirit energy. A bear claw beneath the shirt or wrapping a subtle piece of fur around their rattle handle would be acceptable.

The shaman believes they are talking to guides; perhaps spirits and those spirits have the ability to help them heal. In order to heal, the shaman must be able to connect with the recipient of the healing. This means the recipient of healing needs to be open to receiving it.

---

[213] shamanicdrumming.com, ShamanicDrumming.
[214] Wikipedia, Torma.
[215] buddhaweekly.com/, linterview-bon-teacher-chaphur-rinpoche-explains-bon-different-similar-five-buddhist-schools-tibet.

If a shaman hasn't aligned with practices and rituals of a particular culture, preferring to belong to the one of their birth, they are considered to be contemporary shaman and need to be authentic and be able to communicate this to the recipient and for the information to be accepted.

Direct connection with the spirits is through song and dance. The rhythm of the music, song, and dance takes the shaman into a state of ecstasy where he, or she, is in direct communion with the spirits; they go beyond ordinary human existence and reach a transcendental state of simultaneous existence in this world and the next, and bring him back with messages and information. They also close the session with the spirits and his soul returns to him.

32.1. Drums and Drumstick

Usually the shaman's drum is a fixture of their healing ceremonies and has special qualities. It has been blessed by the shaman, who owns and uses it exclusively. A spirit may exist in the drum that helps the shaman in releasing part of his soul into the journeys he undertakes when it is used. Drumming has a specific role to play in a ceremony.

A slow repetitive drumming rhythm with a frequency close to that measured from the earth has proved effective for the majority of people. It helps induce a range of ecstatic trance states in order to connect with the spiritual dimension of reality. Practised in diverse cultures around the planet, this drum method is strikingly similar to the world over.

Just the way a soothing song can help someone achieve a calmer state. The rhythm of the drum puts you in the right state to journey. The drum beat used is very close to the frequency that is measured from the earth, and has proved effective for the majority of people.

As the Shaman transits through different trance states, the drumming rhythm changes. Eventually the shaman reaches the level necessary for healing to take place. The drumming tempo will change and slow down when the shaman is preparing to leave the trance state. The change in tempo helps draw their consciousness back to normal.

Power animal drumming is a shamanic way to evoke and internalize animal archetypes. An animal archetype represents the spirit and attributes of the entire species of that animal. Shamanism is the endeavour to cultivate ongoing relationships with power animals to gain insight, healing methods, and other vital information that can benefit the community. When an animal spirit is invoked, there is often an accompanying rhythm that comes through. Shamans frequently use these unique rhythms to summon their helping spirits for the work at hand. 216

32.2. Songs

The most important thing about a shamanic song is whether it is effective.

The purpose of the shamanic song is to connect to and bring in different energies. The purpose of the singing that song is to shift one's state of mind and the state of the group that is singing. The song doesn't have to be beautiful, or perfectly written. The power of the song is the doorway that opens between the shaman or the individuals and the power of the spirit world. That doorway is actually open by the singer(s), not the song itself. Some songs are more effective at helping you open that door.[217]

Shamanic songs can be unique to individual healers and/or groups of people; they really aren't different from any spiritual song. Often, the shaman will go to the spirit world to obtain the lyrics or melody of the song. They may have an occasion or a purpose and they will consult with the spirit world to be inspired by a song that fits well with what they want to do.

In terms of spiritual practice, there are many healthful benefits to singing and positive purposes for singing. Here are some of those benefits: [218]

---

[216] shamanicdrumming.com, ShamanicDrumming.
[217] shamanlinks.net, SingingShamanicSongs-ShamanLinks.
[218] shamanlinks.net, SingingShamanicSongs-ShamanLinks.

- Singing is a very powerful way of filling yourself with good energy.
- Singing can help you change your emotions, or your state of mind.
- Shamans use songs to help groups harmonize their energy with one another.
- Singing can help you connect with a higher power, such as angels, or guardian spirits, or the divine (in whatever way you name it).
- You can use singing to bring good energy into a room. In some spiritual practices, songs are used to invoke or invite. For instance, there are songs for rain, or songs for inviting a power animal to be with you.
- Many shamans have a healing song that they sing when they work with their clients.
- Songs can be used to bless another person or a group of people.
- Singing can connect you to the deeper knowing that is inside of you.
- Songs can help you release or express feelings or stuck energies you have found it difficult to release or express by thinking or talking about them.
- Songs are capable of healing you.

32.3. Dance

Dance is a creative activity. A shaman will add dance to their drumming and singing to bring spirits into our world. These are spirits they have asked their helping spirits to bring for the purposes of healing. Physically moving the human body requires energy and coordination and strongly reinforces the request and connection. It adds a mutual energy exchange between the shaman and the spirits they are dancing with.

When the spirit is an animal, certain steps, and actions during the dance will mimic and imply the spirit of the animal the shaman is connected with.

Dance is also a traditional element of spiritual practice. The intention and form of the dance may have a specific purpose. A dance may start as a method of connecting to and invoking spirits for the healing that is requested. Later, towards the end of the dance, the message to the spirits is maybe one of thanks for attending and participating in the ceremony.

Some shaman will dance because they enjoy dancing with their spirits and guides and this personal connection through motion and energy is an important way to express and enjoy their connection.

32.4. Costumes

All parts of the costume are personal to the shaman. A shaman's costume is not bought off the shelf; it is made on the direction of the spirits and the spirit world the shaman journeys to. It is made of time and may have things added to it and taken away depending on the humanizing the shaman is undertaking.

The other aspect of the costume is the self-training wearing the costume instilled on the shaman. By putting on the costume, they are communicating to themselves the role they are taking on, the power they are seeking to accept and connect with and also the start of the session. By taking it off, they are leaving the session and the connection.

32.5. Head Band and Head Dress

Feathers symbolize flight, travel, and the ability of the shaman to travel with and to the spirits he or she must visit in the upper or lower worlds to discover the cause of what is afflicting the recipient and how healing is to be achieved. Feathers from powerful birds, especially predators such as Eagles, instill power into the headdress and the shaman's connection to these animals.

If the shaman's power animal is a bird, feathers, or claws of the bird are an essential part of the headdress and show honour and the state of their connectedness because the shaman is wearing aspects of the physical animal.

Other symbols can be communicated in the head dress. The four seasons, the four directions certain elements. Parts of the Shamanic cosmos can also appear. Even the DNA spiral can be added to a modern shaman's head dress and head band.

A head band may have cords or tassels hanging down which cover the face and form a screen which prevents people from seeing the shaman's face. There are three reasons usually offered for this:

1. The shaman will take on the characteristics of their helping spirit or guide. This may include the face of a guide that has long since passed over. People seeing this altered face would / might be scared. The screen hides the face of the spirit from onlookers.

2. The cords and tassels symbolize the nature of the two worlds. The physical world is on our side of the cord screen; the shaman is on the other side, soul journeying in another realm.

3. Distraction. The screen removes the physical world from the shaman's gaze, removing what is taking place around him, allowing him to blend and connect with the spirit world more effectively.

32.6. Cloak

As with the head dress and head band, there are no strict guidelines on how to build and what should be represented on such a shamanic garment. It should include more connections to their power animal and spirits they are connected with. This may mean duplicating some aspects of the head dress and head band, but reinforcement of these helping spirits is very acceptable.

They are allies and helpers in the spirit world, expressing the connection cannot be done too often!

The cloak also represents energy, a shield against harmful or malevolent spirits the shaman may encounter. Some shaman, at the direction of their helping spirits may attach panels of highly polished metal to their cloak. The metal acts as a mirror.

A malevolent spirit seeking to attack the shaman will see themselves in the mirror and become confused and leave. Metal is used because a piece of an actual mirror may break and become useless. Shards of glass are also dangerous to the shaman if the malevolent spirt finds a way to use a piece to attack the shaman. Bells and metal made to rattle can be attached to scare away harmful spirits.

32.7. Foot Wear

During shamanizing, dancing, and soul journeying, strong, protective footwear is required! Footwear, usually some sort of boots, can be decorated with symbols and elements of power animals, helping spirits and guides. Something along the lines of these boots will bring me home. But also, if during a soul journey the shaman must cross a river, walk on water, or across rough ground, suitable footwear is required.

32.8. Alters and Shrines

Alters and shrines in a home or shamanic place of healing reinforce the shamans power animals, and all helping spirits. Metal mirrors may be on display to ward off and confuse any dark or lower spirits which may seek to harm the shaman as he prays.

Members of the shaman's family may be represented, especially if those family members were shamans; their energy and strength can be called on to help the living shaman. Food offering and offerings of other acceptable gifts to the spirits will be displayed and available for the spirits to consume.

Representation of local spirits associated with the spiritual beings of the area where the shaman is living will be important. When humans build houses or even set down a temporary abode, we disrupt the spirits in the local area. By showing them on the altar, we honour them and ask for their agreement to us staying there.

33. Shamanic Mirrors

Shamanic mirrors are metallic discs made of bronze or other metals, polished on one side, their "face" and usually decorated on the "back." In the centre of the back, there is often a knob or boss with a hole through it. This hole is to allow a cord, silk ribbon, or scarf to be passed through it, which enables the mirror to be suspended or tied to a costume, hung over a shaman alter, or, if small enough, attached to a shaman's costume. The cord, ribbon, or scarf allows the mirror to be handled without torching the polished reflective surface.

The face of a bronze mirror is generally convex, although some are flat. Concave mirrors are rare. Historically, in ancient China household fires were kept alive both day and night throughout the year to cook, heat water and for warmth. However, once a year, the fires had to be put out. The next day, at noon, new fires were ceremonially lit by a shaman or priest, who used a concave bronze mirror. When using such a mirror, the sun's rays are reflected into a single point, which generates enough heat to light some kindling. Today we can achieve the same result by the use of a glass lens. Himalayan melong[219] mirrors, with a bronze loop on their top edge, are sometimes polished on both sides. These are convex on the one face, and concave on the other. As a heart protecting mirror, the convex side is worn outward. For divination purposes, the convex side is to see into the future, and the concave side to see into the past.[220]

The origin of ceremonial mirrors developed in Neolithic times with the art of grinding and polishing stone. Obsidian and jade were often used in ancient mirrors, and these stones are found in different locations around the world, such as Mexico, Anatolia, and China. Polished, iron-rich meteorites may also predate cast bronze mirrors, and these have been used for a very long time in Tibet to create mirrors and other sacred objects.

Over the millennia, shamans have found many ways to use their mirrors. Some shaman mirrors are often known as toli[221] and give spirits a house to live in. Some shamans use them by entering a trance and working with the energies amplified by, or inherently present, in the mirror. Shamans use them for performing healings, for exorcism and for soul retrieval.

A toli is a round, ritual mirror used in Shamanism in some parts of Mongolia and in the Republic of Buryatia. The mirror, ornamented on one side with depictions of animals, plants, birds and polished on the other, may be made of bronze, brass, or copper.

Small Toli is traditionally worn as part of a shaman's attire around the shaman's neck, or in quantity on the shaman's kaftan or apron, which is often referred to as their armour. These pieces of ritual clothing help to protect the shaman from hostile spirit attack. Toli helps ward off harmful or attacking spirits in their own right, and can also be thought of as an object which signifies the shaman's authority or role.[222]

One role of the Toli is as heart protector. The toli must be large enough to cover a shaman's heart and the cord, scarf, or ribbon must be long enough for the mirror to rest over the heart, a vital organ, and one that evil spirits will attack. Smaller mirrors, just a few centimetres across, may be attached to the shaman's costume or be set into wooden handles, which the shaman can hold. The belief is that an evil spirt will see their reflection in the mirror and be terrified and run away.

When a shaman dies, it is traditional for their body, mirror[s], drum[s] and other sacred items to be taken to a remote location and set out on a platform in a tree. Later generations of shamans may accidentally "find" the deceased's mirrors and other bronze objects, and after consulting the spirit of the deceased shaman to ask for permission to adopt the mirror, the shaman who found these ancient objects could use them in his own work.

Himalayan melong[223] mirrors, with a bronze loop on their top edge, are sometimes polished on both sides. These are convex on the one face, and concave on the other.[224]

---

[219] Wikipedia, Melong.
[220] http://www.greenshinto.com/wp/2016/03/12/zen-and-shinto-10-more-mirrors/, ZenandShinto ShamanMirrorsGreenShinto.
[221] Wikipedia, Tolishamanism.
[222] Wikipedia, Tolishamanism.
[223] Wikipedia, Melong.
[224] http://www.greenshinto.com/wp/2016/03/12/zen-and-shinto-10-more-mirrors/, ZenandShinto ShamanMirrorsGreenShinto.

Tibetan Buddhism or Lamaism is a blend of Buddhism that entered Tibet in the eighth century and shamanism. The unique blend found in Tibet has followers in Mongolia, China, and Nepal. In this tradition, mahasiddhas[225] great adepts or mystics, oracles and healers all have melongs or "heart protecting mirrors."

A. Mahasiddha is someone who embodies and cultivates the "siddhi[226] of perfection." A siddha[227] is an individual who attains the realization of siddhis, psychic and spiritual abilities and powers. Mahasiddhas were practitioners of yoga and Tantra, or tantrikas. Their historical influence throughout the Indian subcontinent and the Himalayas was vast and they reached mythic proportions as codified in their songs of realization and hagiographies, or namtars, many of which have been preserved in the Tibetan Buddhist canon. The Mahasiddhas are the founders of Vajrayana[228] traditions and lineages, such as Dzogchen[229] and Mahamudra.[230]

The 9th-century Borobudur stupa in Java shows the Buddha surrounded by monks, who lift their handled mirrors, so as to charge them with the high energy of his enlightened being.
This use of mirrors as a sort of "sacred battery" which holds a spiritual charge also occurs in medieval Europe, as Christian relics were sometimes viewed in a mirror, the mirror capturing and holding the reflection of the sacred relic for the pilgrim to take away with them.[231]

Large alter mirrors are displayed on Buddhist alters to symbolize radiant emptiness. A shaman will display their alter mirror on their shamanic alter because it is the honoured home of their helping spirits, and as a symbol of their shamanic power.

Shamanic ritual mirrors are living things. Not only do they contain helping spirits but also a master spirit. The mirror is cleaned, stored, and also dressed according to the instructions of the Master Spirit. Listening to the mirror will result in instructions on how to work with it and the spirits to which it is home. This includes any offerings they require. Traditional offerings to mirrors are incensed, juniper or sage smoke, alcohol—generally vodka—songs and the sounds of drums rattles and bells.[232] In Mongolia, shamans mirrors were, and still are, blooded in the blood of a sacrificed sheep. The blood is said to transfer the life force of the animal to the mirror.

A shamanic mirror is dressed in silk. The colours of the silk represent both the five elements and the sacred directions. Spirits may request additional offerings to be attached to their mirror, such as beads, stones, shells, or small bells too.

Bronze is an alloy of copper and tin. The percentage of tin varies from between 10% and 30%. The tin content changes the colour and hardness of the bronze; for example, a high level of tin makes the mirror brittle, and it will be prone to break easy, whereas a low level of tin gives a warm red shine, but will easily oxidize. A mirror that is brittle is not desirable. If an evil spirit confronts the shaman, it could break or shatter the mirror, leaving the shaman without heart protection. For this

---

[225] Wikipedia, Mahasiddha.
[226] Wikipedia, Siddhi.
[227] Wikipedia, Siddha.
[228] The Mirror, 'TheTibetanBookoftheDead'andVajrayana.
[229] Wikipedia, Dzogchen.
[230] Wikipedia, Mahasiddha.
[231] http://www.greenshinto.com/wp/2016/03/12/zen-and-shinto-10-more-mirrors/, ZenandShinto ShamanMirrorsGreenShinto.
[232] http://www.greenshinto.com/wp/2016/03/12/zen-and-shinto-10-more-mirrors/, ZenandShinto ShamanMirrorsGreenShinto.

reason, glass is also not used as part of a shaman's mirror. A mirror that has oxidized will affect its reflectivity and, therefore, its ability to scare away an evil spirit when it sees its reflection.

Gold, silver, lead and sometimes zinc, can be added to the bronze, which all influence the resulting bronze medal. In the Tibetan language, there are five different words for bronze. Incorporating metal donated by the shaman, who will use the mirror, creates a bond between the mirror and the shaman practitioner.

34. Shamanism: Changing Perceptions

As noted in the sections on Witch Doctors and Medicinal People, they are not shaman; calling any other indigenous traditional healer a shaman is also not correct. The shamans discussed and their heritage is in Tibet, Nepal, and on the Mongolian Plain as well as Siberia.

In those regions, the shamans have filled many roles through history. In their societies, they have been a traditional healer, a spiritual leader, ritualist, soul guide, sacrificer, song reciter, dancer, and a dramatic performer, confident and even a tribal leader.

In a trance, they would journey to other realms, sometimes dangerous and threatening realms. On those journeys, they were guided by spirits and animals; they retrieved souls that had become lost or even stolen. They journeys to find and discover the cause of illness and how to remedy and heal the recipient.

These abilities, ceremonies, and paraphernalia have made shaman targets for persecution and mistreatment as "modern" western religions connected with shamans. Drums, ceremonial clothing, and all evidence of the shaman's ability were burned and destroyed; baptism was enforced.

Perhaps worse, denigration of shamans as lesser people, themselves by calling them by disrespectful names and labels, such as devils and demons, and assigning them a lower rank or status in society.

The twentieth century misapplication of the word shaman to other cultural heritages denigrates the word and the societies to which it rightfully applies as well as those it does not.

Persecution of Siberian shamans and prohibition of shamanic ceremonies began in 17th century Siberia at the time orthodox Christianity was forced on the population. Yet, it failed to eradicate shamanism; many Russians, even czarist officials, turned to shamanic practitioners for advice and assistance and availed themselves of the shaman's otherworldly capabilities.

Declining religious influence, especially Judo-Christian churches, in the Western world, has coincided with the realignment of shamanism by scientific investigation and reporting, who now sees the shaman as a neuropsychiatric healer.

During a shamanic ceremony, the shaman will enter an altered state of consciousness [ASC]. The ASC is often referred to as an ecstatic state. It is during this time that they connect with the other realms they are journeying to, their helping spirits and the gods and spirits, that will help them help the recipient, on whose behalf they are making this journey.

The ecstatic state also describes a dislocation between the physical individual that is the shaman in the ceremony and the soul of a person journeying to another realm. The ASC or trance state allows the shaman to journey from their physical existence to the destination they need to go. This may involve flying that transforms themselves into a bird or riding on an animal. In this journey, there is no restriction on which of the worlds they can go to; upper, middle for lower. They simply go where they are needed or choose to go.

Lower world journeys are usually in cases of soul retrieval, or bring a dead person's soul to Erleg Khan.

A common metaphor for a journey such as this is an Out of Body experience commonly reported by many people. In an out-of-body experience, their two souls or beings exist: the physical one and the ephemeral one that can journey across the room, look at a room from a different perspective or across the world. Military forces, notably the US and Russians, have experimented with "remote viewing" of each other's secret sites and have done so for decades.

In shamanic ceremonies, the ASC state is self-induced by the shaman and western medical background has frequently attributed psychopathology from actions and expressions of shamanic practitioners in such an ASC; of shaman candidates during their initiatory period and of performing shamans during their ceremonies.

During an ASC trance, a shaman may utter animal sounds as transformations into different spirits occur. He/She may appear unconscious in this world, as certain stages of the journey take place. If the shaman is dancing or drumming, the speed and rhythm may change according to the progress made.

Most Altaic[233] shamans speak of passing nine landmarks during their journey regardless of which world they travel in.

Most traditional non-Western cultures and in historical European cultures, ASC are or was interpreted either as a special state of the individual permitting of close interaction with supernatural entities, in order to receive their messages, perceive them in visions, and acquire power from them; or as a state of possession in which a supernatural entity or power acts through the individual.[234]

It is worth noting at this point that the shaman is not possessed. Shamanism is not a possession state belief. Shamanic possession is not actually possession at all, but the intentional embodiment of spirit helps with whom the shaman has already developed a working relationship. Possession is unintentional intrusion of a foreign spirit into a person, which is considered an energetic illness or unhealthy state in shamanism. Embodiment is an effective, working, altered state the shaman is able to begin and end at will.
Shamanism and possession nonetheless share biological features in their elicitation of ancient brain systems to modify consciousness in relation to healing and spiritual experiences.

Shamans are chosen by a spirit, or the demonstrate the ability to connect with the other realms and spirits but have no reference to do so and no way of organizing and managing what is happening to them. This is not a role people can vie for like a class president. There is no written exam mark to be passed. Initiatory sickness, as it is called, takes many forms depending on the person being called and their circumstances. Nervous fits, attacks of insanity, loss of consciousness, epileptic convulsions and experiences of being torn apart or dismembered are some of them. In the 2000s, the experience and reference points will be different from those of hundreds of years ago. Recovery from the sickness is presented by shaman teachers as a form of death and rebirth; being reborn to the shamanic vocation as a changed person.[235]

---

[233] Wikipedia, Altaiclanguages.
[234] Wolfgang G. Jilek, TransformingtheShamanChangingWesternViewsofShamanismandAlteredStatesofConsciousness.
[235] Jilek, TransformingtheShamanChangingWesternViewsofShamanismandAlteredStatesofConsciousness.

On the individual and interpersonal level, shamanic practitioners, unlike Western-trained health professionals, combine the confidence-inspiring reputation of a charismatic personality with access to supernatural powers and a culture-congenial understanding of their clients' belief and value system. [236]

All this may explain the survival of shamanic practices among indigenous peoples in spite of centuries of suppression by governmental and ecclesiastical authorities. However, beyond mere survival, we witness a revival of shamanic healing rituals and ceremonialism, especially among North American indigenous populations under Westernizing acculturation pressure. This indigenous renaissance is reflected in the revitalization of traditional ceremonials with important therapeutic aspects throughout North America.

Examples are the Winter Spirit Dances of the Salish in the Pacific Northwest; the Sun Dance among aboriginal populations of Wyoming, Idaho, Utah, Colorado, and the Dakotas; the Gourd Dance among the Kiowa, Comanche, Cheyenne, and Arapaho, which subsequently reached many other tribes in the United States and Canada; the Peyote Cult, which spread northward from Mexico and is today a major pan-Amerindian religious ceremonial east of the Rocky Mountains. [237]

In North America, the expansion of rituals and ceremonies speaks to the need for indigenous people to have an identity unique and special to themselves. Preserving and expanding the role of traditional healers is a powerful way of expressing this voice while allowing for modern medicine to intervene where necessary.

In reading and exploring the role of Tibetan Shaman and Shamanism at the roof of the world. Shaman there do not diagnose and will send a potential client to a doctor to get antibiotics or more expensive treatment.

Beginning in the later part of the 1900s, what we call "New Age" shamanism has appeared and taken hold in people and places without the indigenous or traditional heritage associated with shamanism.

This profound and honest interest in shamanism in cultures that do not have a historical connection to shamanism is due to an enquiring mind and desire to understand and the feeling that there is more to what I know and understand. Shamanism would not have survived from the Paleolithic without it having a substance to it.

The revival of shamanic ceremonialism is one aspect of the renaissance of indigenous culture. It is no coincidence this occurred in the aftermath of decolonization, accompanied by a profound change of the prevailing Western attitudes after World War II. There has been a change in the world view and sense of superiority. No longer is Europe or North America the centre for everything that is right and correct, and prepared to remake everything in their image. Today they are the source of financial resources, powerful inquisitiveness, and a desire to explore and understand.

---

[236] Jilek, TransformingtheShamanChangingWesternViewsofShamanismandAlteredStatesofConsciousness.
[237] Jilek, TransformingtheShamanChangingWesternViewsofShamanismandAlteredStatesofConsciousness.

35. Persecution of Shaman

35.1. Religious Persecution in Tibet

Current religious persecution in Tibet does not stem from ethnic or religious conflict or discrimination by a majority against a minority. It is politically motivated, and consciously applied to realize political and military ends.

35.2. History

The Tibetan Plateau has been inhabited by humans for at least 21,000 years. The Neolithic period saw immigrants from northern China largely displace the humans around 3,000 years ago. There remains some genetic continuity between the Paleolithic inhabitants and contemporary Tibetan populations.[238]

The earliest Tibetan historical texts identify the Zhang Zhung culture as a people who migrated from the Amdo region into what is now the region of Guge in western Tibet. Zhang Zhung is considered to be the original home of the Bon religion.

By the first century BCE—Before Common Era[239], a neighbouring kingdom arose in the Yarlung Valley, and the Yarlung king, Drigum Tsenpo, attempted to remove the influence of the Zhang Zhung by expelling the Zhang Bon priests from Yarlung. He was assassinated and Zhang Zhung continued its dominance of the region until it was annexed by Songtsen Gampo in the seventh century. Prior to Songtsen Gampo, the kings of Tibet were more mythological than factual, and there is insufficient evidence of their existence.

The fall of the Tibetan Empire[240] resulted in the region breaking up into a variety of territories each controlled by a warlord with overall influence being either Mongol or Chinese but with a reasonable amount of self-determination and flexibility. Eventually, with the fall of the Mongol empire and influence, Tibet was absorbed into the Chinese provinces of Sichuan and Qinghai. Generally, the current borders of Tibet were determined by the 18th century.

In 1950, The Peoples Republic of China negotiated an agreement with the newly enthroned 14th Dalai Lama affirming China's sovereignty over Tibet. Autonomy Created the Tibetan Autonomous Regional [TAR] and the head of the government to be ethnic Tibetan. In reality, the actual power in the TAR is the First Secretary of the Tibetan Autonomous Regional Committee of the Chinese Communist Party, who has never been a Tibetan. The role of ethnic Tibetans in the higher levels of the TAR Communist Party remains very limited.

In exile, the Dalai Lama[241] repudiated the agreement. Many Tibetans have fled Tibet to Nepal and India. The Dalai Lama has a strong following; many Tibetans look at him as both a political and a spiritual leader.

---

[238] Wikipedia, Tibet.
[239] Wikipedia, CommonEra.
[240] Wikipedia, TibetanEmpire.
[241]

A rival Tibetan government-in-exile, The Central Tibetan Administration, also referred to as The Tibetan Government in Exile, is located in India. Its internal structure is government-like; it has stated that it is "not designed to take power in Tibet"; rather, it will be dissolved as soon as freedom is restored in Tibet in favour of a government formed by Tibetans inside Tibet. In addition to political advocacy, it administers a network of schools and other cultural activities for Tibetans in India. [242]

During the Chinese Cultural Revolution[243] 1959–1961, most of Tibet's more than 6,000 monasteries were destroyed and others severely damaged and defaced by the Communist Party of China and monastic estates were broken up and secular education introduced.[244] During this period, religious objects, of any sort, were confiscated and destroyed, removing a significant amount of personally owned history and connection with the past heritage of Tibet.

Restrictions were lifted during the 1980s as a result of a period of relative accommodation but it resulted in a resurgence of religious activity both formal and public as well as personal; Tibetans created altars in their homes, prayed in public, and made pilgrimages to holy places. Rebuilding of temples and monasteries—almost entirely supported by people's voluntary labour and resources. Those monasteries and nunneries were filled with young monks and nuns who wished to pursue a religious vocation in spite of growing up under Communist Chinese rule.

In 1987 and subsequent years, the arrest of monks, nuns, and the display of images of the Dali Lama, shouting slogans and putting up posters have been instituted. Subsequent economic and other reforms have sought to suppress religious activity and any visible reference to the Dali Lama as a spiritual or political head of Tibet.

35.3. Shamans

Shamanism is the oldest religious activity in humanity; it was and has been effected in two ways.

First, in a community, a Shaman is a highly respected and honoured confident, healer, and leader. In both Soviet Russia and China, those roles can be manipulated into a portrayal of the shaman as an oppressor of this tribe or community. They were seen to fall into the same classification as land owners, merchants, local leaders, or aristocracy. In both Soviet Russia and China, Shamans were purged, arrested, tortured, and shot along with the other classes of people communist forces saw as being oppressors and inhibiting progress of socialist ideas and disrupting the agricultural and societal changes they wanted to make in the name of state ownership.

Suppression by the Red Army and the People's Liberation Army [China] included not just the shaman, but possessions, all things that formed the shaman's heritage and places of worship. And performance of rituals. Some interesting workarounds to survive the persecution have been recorded. One Shaman in Siberia turned his rituals into what he called a "theatre production." In this way, he was providing entertainment rather than say a soul retrieval ritual, if anyone from the local Soviet happened to be in the "audience" and wanted to know. Other Shamans survived by simply being in very remote locations that the communist re-educators and military did not care to go.

---

[242] Wikipedia, CentralTibetanAdministration.
[243] Wikipedia, CulturalRevolution.
[244] Wikipedia, CulturalRevolution.

In both Soviet Russia and Tibet, the systematic state sponsored destruction of monasteries and arrest of monks and nuns was material to deprive their respective societies of the physical presence of shamans, Bonpo, and Buddhist monks as well as the physical presence of buildings and places of worship.

The heritage and substance of shamanism, which had been part of a chain of religious growth, through Bon and ultimately into Tibetan Buddhism with its scholarly monastic environment where practices and beliefs were recorded in books and scripture, was unlike any persecution that had come and gone previously.

The introduction of Russian and Chinese languages with state education to replace shamanic teachings and monastic education has resulted in more than one generation growing up without any connection to traditional shamanic teaching, training, and practices, or monastic Buddhist teachings. However, as noted previously, this did not prevent people of all ages attempting reconnection with their spiritual and religious heritage.

Since the collapse of the Soviet system in 1991, there has been a resurgence of Shamanic activity in The Mongolian People's Republic. To the point where Shamans advertise, they can be members of the Corporate Union of Mongolian Shamans, appear on television and run for local administrative political positions.

However, the loss of people, Shamans, men and women who provided a physical presence and their oral history along with their costumes, drums, altars, and all their paraphernalia cannot be replaced, just as the heritage in the monasteries destroyed by the Chinese communists cannot be replaced.

There are two key differences between the resurgence of Shamanism in Mongolia and Tibet. First, Mongolia is free to determine its own path, and make its own laws and regulations. Second is the deep and magnetic reverence for Chinggis Khan, or Genghis Khan,[245] and the achievement of the Mongol people during the Mongolian Empire is genuine and a source of pride and self-identity.

35.4. Current Threats

Persecution in Soviet Russia and Communist China was systematic, organized, and state sponsored. Shamanism faces new forms of denigration and persecution.

Changes are needed to Western notions of shamanism, the shamanic healer, and the role of altered states of consciousness (ASC). Before the Age of Enlightenment, the shaman was condemned as demoniac charlatan. From the mid-19th until the mid-20th century, the shaman was generally considered as being afflicted with a psychiatric or epileptic condition; a notion based on the misinterpretation of altered states of consciousness in shamanic rituals as psychopathological. [246]

It is worth noting at this point that the shaman is not possessed. Shamanism is not a possession-based belief. Shamanic possession is not actually possession at all, but the intentional embodiment of spirit helps with whom the shaman has already developed a working relationship.

---

[245] Wikipedia, GenghisKhan.
[246] Jilek, TransformingtheShamanChangingWesternViewsofShamanismandAlteredStatesofConsciousness.

Possession is unintentional intrusion of a foreign spirit into a person who is considered an energetic illness or unhealthy state in shamanism. Embodiment is an effective, working, altered state the shaman is able to begin and end at will.

Shamanism and possession nonetheless share biological features in their elicitation of ancient brain systems to modify consciousness in relation to healing and spiritual experiences.

The word shaman has been misapplied to other indigenous healers. This was covered in detail in the first book of a Shaman series. A Shaman is not a Witch Doctor, nor is the Shaman a Medicine Man/Woman.

Neoshamanism refers to "new" forms of shamanism, or methods of seeking visions or healing. Neoshamanism comprises an eclectic range of beliefs and practices that involve attempts to attain altered states and communicate with a spirit world. Neoshamanic systems may not resemble traditional forms of shamanism. Some have been invented by individual practitioners, though many borrow or gain inspiration from a variety of different indigenous cultures. In particular, indigenous cultures of the Americas have been influential. [247]

Neoshamanism is not a single, cohesive belief system, but a collective term for many philosophies and activities. However, certain generalities may be drawn between adherents. Most believe in spirits and pursue contact with the "spirit world" in altered states of consciousness, which they achieve through drumming, dance, or the use of entheogens. Most systems might be described as existing somewhere on the animism/pantheism spectrum. Some neoshamans are not trained by any traditional shaman or member of any American indigenous culture, but rather learn independently from books and experimentation. Many attend New Age workshops and retreats, where they study a wide variety of ideas and techniques, both new and old.[248]

Some members of traditional, indigenous cultures and religions are critical of Neoshamanism, asserting that it represents an illegitimate form of cultural appropriation, or that it is nothing more than a ruse by fraudulent spiritual leaders to disguise or lend legitimacy to fabricate, ignorant, and/or unsafe elements in their ceremonies.

According to York (2001), one difference between neoshamanism and traditional shamanism is the role of fear. Neoshamanism and its New Age relations tend to dismiss the existence of evil, fear, and failure. "In traditional shamanism, the shaman's initiation is an ordeal involving pain, hardship, and terror. New Age, by contrast, is a religious perspective that denies the ultimate reality of the negative, and this would devalue the role of fear as well."[249]

Inaccurate representation, misrepresentation and careless referencing, attributing actions and belief systems to what is truly a shaman are a danger to shamans everywhere.

---

[247] Wikipedia, Neoshamanism.
[248] Wikipedia, Neoshamanism.
[249] Wikipedia, Neoshamanism.

36. Asian and European Shamanism

36.1. Humming Shamanism

The Hmong is an ancient Chinese people they have a history going back over 5,000 years. Today they continue their Ua Neeb shamanic practices. To a Hmong shaman, there is their main job, their reason for existence and the soul path purpose they were destined to follow. Their rituals and beliefs invoke trance to bring harmony to the individual, family, and community.

At the end of the Vietnam War, 200,000 Hmong were resettled in the United States and continued to practise shamanism there. The Hmong practice animal sacrifice as part of their shamanic rituals. Animal sacrifice has been part of their rituals for over 5,000 years. Animal sacrifice is not a brutal killing a helpless animal; the sacrificial animals and the process of taking life are treated with great respect and care. However, animal sacrifice is not part of American life and as a result The Hmong have found themselves in a number of court cases and friction with authorities as a result.

The Hmong believes that all things on Earth have a soul, or multiple souls. The souls are equal and interchangeable. Sickness is believed to be the result of a person's soul being lost or captured by a wild spirit; the animal to be sacrificed is asked to give up its soul in exchange for that of the suffering individual. This is to be for 12 months. During the Hmong New Year ceremonies, the shaman performs a ritual to release the soul of that animal, where it is sent to the world beyond and the soul is also reincarnated at a higher level or even becomes part of God's family and lives a life of luxury, free of animal suffering. Undertaking this sacrifice and service is a very high honour for the animal.

Hmong shaman also attempts to treat physical illnesses through use of sacred words—khawv koob.

36.1. Japan

Shamanism is part of the indigenous Ainu religion and, more broadly, Shinto. Shinto is distinct in that its shamanism is for an agricultural society.

From the Early Middle Ages, Shinto has been influenced by religious practices from East Asian shamanism or Shinto. Most particularly, it has been affected by Buddhism.

36.2. S. Korea

Shamanism is still practised in North and South Korea.

In South Korea, shamans are almost entirely female. The name for an S. Korean Shaman is Mudang; male shamans are referred to as basso mudang. A person can become a shaman through hereditary title or through natural ability.

Shamans are consulted in contemporary society for financial and marital decisions. As noted in book 1 of this series, S. Korean Mudangs are highly costumed and rituals are performed both privately and as a theatrical performance. Mudangs are accompanied by musicians, singers and often a stage or platform on which the ritual is performed for a usually seated audience.

36.3. Malaysia

Shamanism is practised by the Malay community on the Malay Peninsula and by indigenous people in Sabah and Sarawak.

People who practise shamanism in the country are generally called bomoh or pawang in the Peninsula. In Sabah, the Bobohizan is the main shaman among the Kadazan-Dusun indigenous community.

36.4. Mongolia

Mongol Shamans historically and today may be male or female and fill many roles in Mongol society. Exorcisms, healers, rainmakers, oneiromancers, soothsayers, and as members of the Corporate Union of Mongolian Shamans, run for public office, they appear on television and radio, and advertise their services.

As a member of the Mongolian Shamans Association, they can participate in the continued revival of Mongolian Shamanism.

Historically, the clan based Mongol society was complex and the spirit world matched the physical world in its complexity.

The highest spirit group was the 99 Tngri; 55 being benevolent or "white" and 44 terrifying or "black." White and black banners we raised in all Mongolian encampments and both honoured. Because of their fierceness, the black banner and its 44 Tngri rode into any battles the clan or the greater Mongols fought. It was the banner under which Chinggis Khan built the Mongol Empire. It is worth noting that Chinggis Khan, though not a shaman, worshiped and interceded with the black Tngri frequently during his lifetime.

The Tngri was followed by 77 natigai or "earth mothers." Mongolian shamanism incorporates ancestor worship. Chief of the ancestors a shaman may call on is the closely connected wand those by groups of ancestral spirits the "Lord-Spirits" these being the spirits and souls of clan leaders who will provide physical and spiritual help. Next are "Protector-Spirits" these being the souls and spirits of great shamans, male and female. Lesser shamans [male and female] were called "Guardian-Spirits," which were connected to a specific locality, such as a mountain or river belonging to the clan.

In the 1990s, the Soviet system fell. There has been a considerable growth in shamanism and many, many more shamans have appeared. As members of the Corporate Union of Mongolian Shamans or Mongolian Shamans' Association, a modernization of the role of the shaman has taken place. Some Mongolian shamans are now making a business out of their profession and even have offices in the larger towns. At these businesses, a shaman generally heads the organization and performs services such as healing, fortune-telling, and solving all kinds of problems.

This has led traditional shamans among the Buryat Mongols to struggle to re-establish their historical and genetic roots now that Soviet oppression has been lifted.

Another dynamic has been a gradual change in the openness of Mongol shamans to offer insights into the role of a shaman. Seeking to protect their ethnic connection and the basis of their practices. Many organizations such as those mentioned are reticent, even restricting access from western neo and New Age shamans.

36.5. Philippines

Babylons were shamans of ethnic groups of the pre-colonial Philippine islands. They were highly respected in the community being elevated to the status of a pre-colonial noble class.

They specialized in harnessing the unlimited powers of nature and were almost always women or feminized men. They were believed to have spirit guides, by which they could contact and interact with the spirits of the spirit world.

They acted as mediums during rituals and specialized in various practices such as healing, herbalism, divination, or sorcery. They were reputed to be able to bring down an enemy, hence their reputation with divine combat.

Gradual conversion to Islam and the later Spanish colonial forced conversion to Catholicism reduced their influence. They were persecuted vigorously by the Spanish, who burned and destroyed anything associated with indigenous religion and murdered thousands of practitioners.

36.6. Siberia and North Asia

Siberia, north of the Mongols—see Mongolia in this section, is inhabited by many different ethnic groups who observe shamanistic practices. Many classical ethnographic sources of shamanism were recorded among Siberian peoples.

Manchu Shamanism is one of very few shamanist traditions which held official status into the modern era, by becoming one of the imperial cults of the Qing dynasty of China, together with Buddhism, Taoism and traditional Heavenly worship. The Palace of Earthly Tranquility is one of the principal halls of the Forbidden City in Beijing and was partly dedicated to shamanistic rituals. The ritual set-up is still preserved in situ today.

Among the Siberian Chukchis people, a shaman is selected by the spirits. The candidate is possessed by a spirit that demands they assume the role of a shaman. The Buryat has a ritual known as shanar whereby a candidate is consecrated as shaman by another, already—established shaman.

Among several Samoyedic peoples, shamanism is a living tradition also in modern times, especially at groups living in isolation, until recent times.

Table 8 Linguistic Family, People and Type of Shamanism

Linguistic Family	Peoples	Shamanism
Uralic	Samoyedic	Among several Samoyedic people's shamanism was a living tradition into modern times, especially at groups living in isolation until recent times. There were distinguished several types of shamans among Nenets, Enets, and Selkup people. The Nganasan shaman used three different crowns, according to the situation: one for the upper world, one for underneath word and one for the occasion of childbirth.
	Nenets	Several types of shamans distinguished by the world they connected with; upper world, underworld, or the dead
	Nganasan	The last notable shaman rituals and seance were performed and recorded in the 1970s
	Sayan Samoyedic	In the 19th century, a language shift saw the adoption of the neighbouring Turkic People. Today the original language is extinct. Karagas Shamanism is influenced by Abakan-Turkic and Buryat practices and Khalkha Mongol is the largest subgroup of Mongol people.

Closure of the border between Soviet Russia and the People's Republic of China in 1949 sealed many nomadic Tungus groups, including the Evenki that practised shamanism in Manchuria and Inner Mongolia. The last shaman of the Oroqen, Chuonnasuan (Meng Jinfu), died in October 2000.

36.7. Vietnam

In Vietnam, shamans conduct rituals in many of the religious traditions that co-mingle in the majority and minority populations. In their rituals, music, dance, special garments and offerings are part of the performance that surrounds the spirit journey.

Shamanism is part of the Vietnamese religion of worship of mother goddesses. In Vietnam, this ritual practice is called Len dong or also known as hau bong. Hau bong sessions involve artistic elements such as music, singing, dance and the use of costumes.

Hat châu van, from northern Vietnam, is a traditional folk art of northern Vietnam, related to shamanism. The genre is famous for its use in rituals for deity mediumship. Châu van serves two purposes: to help hypnotize the medium for the reception of the deities, and to accompany the medium's actions with appropriate music.

36.8. Other Asian traditions

Jhakri is the common name used for shamans in Sikkim (India) and Nepal.

They exist in many communities. They are influenced by Hinduism, Tibetan Buddhism, Mun and Bon rites.

Shamanism is still widely practised in the Ryukyu Islands Okinawa, Japan, where shamans are known as "Noro" all women and "Yuta." "Noro" generally administers public or communal ceremonies, while "Yuta" focuses on civil and private matters. Shamanism is also practised in a few rural areas in Japan proper. It is commonly believed that the Shinto religion is the result of the transformation of a shamanistic tradition into a religion. Forms of practice vary somewhat in the several Ryukyu islands, so that there is, for example, a distinct Miyako shamanism. [48] Shamanist practices seem to have been preserved in the Catholic religious traditions of aborigines in Taiwan.

36.9. Europe

Some of the prehistoric peoples who once lived in Siberia and other parts of Central and Eastern Asia migrated into other regions, bringing their cultures with them. For example, many Uralic peoples live outside Siberia; however, the original location of the Proto-Uralic peoples and its extent are debated.

Combined phytogeographical and linguistic considerations, such as the distribution of various tree species, and their names in various Uralic languages, suggest that this area was north of Central Ural Mountains and on lower and middle parts of the Ob River. Newer studies suggest an origin in Northeast Asia.

It is suggested the Proto-Uralic language is linked to the Chinese Liao civilization. The ancestors of Hungarian people or Magyars have wandered from their ancestral proto-Uralic area to the Pannonian Basin. Shamanism played an important role in Turko-Mongol mythology.

Tengriism, the major ancient belief among Xiongnu, Mongol and Turkic peoples, Magyars, and Bulgars, incorporates elements of shamanism. There are no practising shamans in current-day Hungary, but their folklore does make reference to shamans.

For more detailed overview of regional forms of Shamanism and regions not covered here, please refer to Wikipedia at this link:

URL: https://en.wikipedia.org/wiki/Regional_forms_of_shamanism

37. Bibliography

Bibliography

. (!!! INVALID CITATION !!!).

Ahmad, Feroz. "The Young Turk Revolution." *Journal of Contemporary History* 3, no. 3 (2016): 19-36. https://doi.org/10.1177/002200946800300302.

Art, Rubin Museum of. "Bon Press Release."

BON RELIGION, CATHOLICS AND SUPERSTITION IN TIBET. "Bon Religion, Catholics and Superstition in Tibet."

Britannica. "Bardo ThöDol Tibetan Buddhist Text."

buddhaweekly.com/. "Iinterview-Bon-Teacher-Chaphur-Rinpoche-Explains-Bon-Different-Similar-Five-Buddhist-Schools-Tibet."

Collection, University of California Press eBook. "The Spiritual Quest." (1982 - 2004).

Colleoni, Aldo. *Mongolian Shamanism*. Italy? Ulaanbaatar: National Research Institutue ; Mongolian Academy of Sciences, 2005.

Dictionary, Merriam-Webster. "Definition of Soul by Merriam-Webster."

Dictionary.com. "Definition of Body at Dictionary.Com."

———. "Incorporeal."

———. "Spirit Definition of Spirit."

Encyclopedia, Chinese Buddhist. "Eight Classes of Gods and Demons."

Encyclopedia.com. "Shamans."

English, Longman Dictionary of Contemporary. "Spirit Meaning of Spirit."

Ermakov, Dmitry. "Bo and Bon - Ancient Shamanic Traditions of Siberia and Tibet in Their Relation to the Teachings of a Central Asian Buddha."

GotQuestions.org. "What Is the Difference between the Soul and Spirit of Man?".

Honolulu, Master Sha Tao Center. "Open Spiritual Channels Soul Language and Translation - Honolulu Tao Healing Soul Healing Energy Healing Master Sha."

http://buryatmongol.org/a-course-in-mongolian-shamanism/the-shaman/becoming-a-shaman/. "Becoming a Shaman."

http://donlehmanjr.com/. "The Tibetan Book of the Dead.Pdf."

http://healerofheartsandminds.com. "Reincarnation, Past Lives, Suffering and the Bible, a Shaman's Views."

http://situgen.blogspot.com/search/label/shaman%27s%20costume. "Shaman's Costume."

http://www.face-music.ch/bi_bid/historyoftengerism.html. "Shamanism Tengerism in Mongolia in English."

http://www.greenshinto.com/wp/2016/03/12/zen-and-shinto-10-more-mirrors/. "Zen and Shinto 10 Shaman Mirrors Green Shinto."

https://en.wikipedia.org/wiki/Buryatia. "Buryatia."

https://en.wikipedia.org/wiki/The_City_of_God. "The City of God."

https://garudashop.com/collections/bonpo-shang-bell. "Bonpo Shang Bell | Traditional Tibetan Instrument."

https://hraf.yale.edu. "Altered States of Consciousness."

https://lissarankin.com, Lissa Rankin. "20 Diagnostic Signs That You're Suffering from Soul Loss."

https://mongolianstore.com/the-black-shamans/. "The Black and White Shamans."

https://spiritualgrowthguide.com/tengri-shamanism/. "Tengri Shamanism - the Deities of Tengrism - Spiritual Growth Guide."

https://www.encyclopedia.com/environment/encyclopedias-almanacs-transcripts-and-maps/ancestors-ancestor-worship. "Ancestors Ancestor Worship.Com."

https://www.energy-shifter.com/shamanism-and-spiritual-techniques.html. "Shamanism, and Soul Retrieval - Spiritual House Cleansing."

https://www.facebook.com/EuropeShamanism/photos/a.186820488859769/560852338123247/?type=3. "Henno Erikson Parks - Posts."

https://www.newdawnmagazine.com/articles/secrets-of-siberian-shamanism. "Secrets of Siberian Shamanism."

https://www.newworldencyclopedia.org/entry/Tengriism. "Tengriism New World Encyclopedia."

https://www.timesofisrael.com/12000-year-old-grave-of-shaman-woman-unearthed-in-galilee/. "12,000-Year-Old Grave of Shaman Woman Unearthed in Galilee the Times of Israel."

https://www.wisdomlib.org. "Antarabhava, AntarāBhava 2 Definitions."

Jilek, Wolfgang G. "Transforming the Shaman Changing Western Views of Shamanism and Altered States of Consciousness."

KatyaFaris.com. "Altered States of Consciousness and Healing in Indigenous Rituals – Katya Faris."

Lionsroar.com. "The Four Points of Letting Go in the Bardo."

Merriam-Webster. "Definition of New Age."

Michael, Henry N. editor, and V. N. Chernetsan. *Studies in Siberian Shamanism.* [Toronto]: Published for the Arctic Institute of North America by University of Toronto Press, 1963.

Mirror, The. "'The Tibetan Book of the Dead' and Vajrayana."

moonhoroscope.com/lunar-birthday. "Lunar Birthday."

Petit, Marc, and Christian Lequindre. *Nepal : Shamanism and Tribal Sculpture.* [Gollion]: Infolio, 2009.

Philosophy, Stanford Encyclopedia of. "Descartes and the Pineal Gland."

Rinchen, Yönsiyebü. "White, Black and Yellow Shamans among the Mongols." *Ultimate Reality and Meaning* 4, no. 2 (1981): 94-102. https://doi.org/10.3138/uram.4.2.94.

Rinpoche, Tenzin Wangyal. "Soul Retrieval and Related Ideas."

———. "Tibetan Soul Retrieval."

Sacredsites.com. "World Pilgrimigae Guide."

Seminar, Tibetan Renaissance. "Bon Background Research from the Tibetan Renaissance Seminar."

shamanicdrumming.com. "Shamanic Drumming."

shamanlinks.net. "Singing Shamanic Songs - Shaman Links."

Theinnervoyage.com. "Soul Retrieval."

themystica.com. "Altered States of Consciousness."

Tibet, Bon: Indigenous Shamanism of. "Bon- Indigenous Shamanism of Tibet."
Wiki, Rigpa. "Eight Classes of Gods and Demons."
Wikipeda. "History of the Location of the Soul."
Wikipedia. "Altaic Languages."
———. "Animal."
———. "Animism."
———. "Asia."
———. "Banjhakri and Banjhakrini."
———. "Bardo."
———. "Bardo Thodol."
———. "Carl Jung."
———. "Carol Zaleski."
———. "Cellular Respiration."
———. "Central Tibetan Administration."
———. "Common Era."
———. "Cultural Revolution."
———. "Dissociation Psychology."
———. "Drepung Monastery."
———. "Dzogchen."
———. "Ensoulment."
———. "Genghis Khan."
———. "Hinduism."
———. "Human Body."
———. "Indra."
———. "Irk Bitig."
———. "Jokhang."
———. "Khanate."
———. "Mahasiddha."
———. "Melong."
———. "Mongols."
———. "Mount Kailash."
———. "Mustafa Kemal AtatüRk."
———. "Neoshamanism."
———. "New Age."
———. "Norbulingka."
———. "Ongon."
———. "Paleolithic."
———. "Potala Palace."
———. "Reincarnation."
———. "Sami People."
———. "The Secret History of the Mongols."
———. "Shamanic Music."
———. "Shamanism."
———. "Siddha."
———. "Siddhi."

———. "Skandha."
———. "Sogyal Rinpoche."
———. "Soul."
———. "Spirit."
———. "Taiga."
———. "Tengrism."
———. "Terton."
———. "Tibet."
———. "Tibetan Buddhism."
———. "Tibetan Empire."
———. "Tngri."
———. "Toli Shamanism."
———. "Torma."
———. "Tungusic Languages."
———. "Turkic Languages."
———. "Veneration of the Dead."
———. "Xiongnu."
———. "Yellow Shamanism."
wingsofchaos.com. "Prologue for Zadkiel."
Woolger, Dr. Roger J. "Beyond Death- Transition and the Afterlife."
www.rigpawiki.org. "Emptiness."
———. "Nyingma Buddhism."